Small Schools
and
Strong Communities

A THIRD WAY OF SCHOOL REFORM

Small Schools
and
Strong Communities

A THIRD WAY OF SCHOOL REFORM

KENNETH A. STRIKE
Foreword by Mary Anne Raywid

Teachers College, Columbia University
New York and London

Published by Teachers College Press, 1234 Amsterdam Avenue, New York, NY 10027

Library of Congress Cataloging-in-Publication Data

Strike, Kenneth A.
  Small schools and strong communities : a third way of school reform / Kenneth A. Strike ; foreword by Mary Anne Raywid.
      p. cm.
  Includes bibliographical references and index.
   ISBN 978-0-8077-5058-2 (pbk. : alk. paper)–ISBN 978-0-8077-5059-9 (hardcover : alk paper)
  1. School size. 2. Educational change. 3. School improvement programs. I. Title.
  LB3012.5.S77 2010
  371.2'07--dc22   2009046864
ISBN 978-0-8077-5058-2 (paper)
ISBN 978-0-8077-5059-9 (hardcover)

Printed on acid-free paper
Manufactured in the United States of America

17 16 15 14 13 12 11 10   8 7 6 5 4 3 2 1

To Maya and Molly,
May their education be communal

Contents

Foreword

In this book, Ken Strike has provided something rare: an intellectual justification for an emphasis that at root is extensively emotional. His "third way" of school reform is to recognize the community that each school becomes as its heart or essence. Community is not solely reducible to strong positive relations, but they play a large part in what shapes and maintains a school. He is right that community is a crucial element of any school—and that it has been essentially overlooked in contemporary reform efforts. Thus Strike's intent to show what it means for schools to be strong communities is as timely as it is important. He is also correct in underscoring that one of the things making small schools so valuable is their potential to create and shape communities. But the connection is really even stronger than that—the small schools movement, he tells us, is articulated by a theory of community as a vision of school reform.

This movement making community so central may presently be just past the peak of its popularity as the major route to school reform. If so, that is a good thing because it may leave fewer people expecting that all you need to do is adopt small schools and good things will start happening. Genuine, lasting school improvement is a bit more complicated and demanding than that. Choosing small schools is a good route to take and represents a highly desirable start, but it is just a first step.

In the pages that follow, Strike has done an excellent job of outlining promising subsequent steps. He has written a book on small schools and done two extremely valuable things with it. He has expanded it into an admirable theory of education—no negligible undertaking. At the same time, he has offered sufficient detail on small schools to suffice as a guide for readers not yet acquainted with what to do to make them succeed. This appears easily the most thorough and detailed extant examination of the way a small school actually works, and I would recommend it to anyone contemplating launching one.

Small Schools and Strong Communities also represents a meticulously reasoned argument. A connection between the two—community on the one hand and small schools on the other—is claimed in Chapter 1, its need and problems are explored in Chapter 2, its existence in Chapter 3, its types in Chapters 4 and 5. Chapter 6 examines the research on small schools and their emphasis on human beings, Chapter 7 deals with good policy for them, and Chapters 8 and 9 contrast small schools—the "third way of school reform"—with the other two more prominent current versions of how to redo public education—via standards and accountability, or via choice. Chapter 10 offers the author's summary and conclusions. Strike makes his case thoroughly and well, and he leaves the reader with few grounds to come away from his book unpersuaded.

Strike manages to cover a lot of ground. He distinguishes good from bad school communities and explores the small schools literature seeing schools as communities before accepting a theory of community as a vision of school reform—presenting quite a contrast with those more prevalent views of school reform that make no mention at all of community!

All in all, *Small Schools and Strong Communities* provides a refreshing look at the school reform scene. It offers novel diagnoses as to what needs fixing in our schools and some unusual prescriptions for cures. It is certainly not just more of the same and is worthy of a serious read.

–Mary Anne Raywid

Acknowledgments

This book began more than 10 years ago with a grant from the Spencer Foundation. The project they funded ended with a set of papers on the topic of schools as communities. But, as I recall, I promised to do a book. At that time the papers somehow refused to gel into a book, so I must thank the Spencer Foundation both for its initial support and its forbearance. They ask that people whose work they support include a statement in what they publish to the effect that the views and ideas they express should not be attributed to them: Hence the Spencer Foundation cannot be held accountable for my views or my errors; they are mine alone.

Two groups of students at Syracuse University and one group at Pennsylvania State University suffered through seminars on this topic with me. I want to thank the students who attended them for their patience with me while I tried out ideas on them and changed my mind about things. They offered many helpful suggestions.

Mary Anne Raywid read the manuscript, offered encouragement, and made many helpful suggestions. My thanks to her. Her work has been a major source of inspiration and ideas for this book. I am most pleased that she seems to like it.

Syracuse University has allowed me to teach part-time there while I finished this book and has treated me as though I was a real faculty member. Thanks to my friends at the Cultural Foundations of Education Department and the College of Education for their friendship and collegiality. Special thanks to Emily Robertson, who made my sojourn at Syracuse possible.

I would also like to thank my wife Joanne for putting up with me while I worked on this. It has interfered with travel, deferred our retirement, cut into our canoeing time, and kept her from her e-mail. I have also imposed on her to proofread this, which she has done with her usual care and thoroughness. I view this as a sign of affection, which I reciprocate.

Thanks also to Teachers College Press for their understanding of the fact that this took longer than I expected and promised and for their work in turning the manuscript into a real book.

Finally I would like to remember the late Tom Green, who was a friend, colleague, and mentor for many years. The idea of "normation" that features prominently in this book is largely his. I'm hopeful that he would be pleased with what I have done with it.

Preface

I don't imagine that anyone will be persuaded by this old Shaker hymn, "Simple Gifts," that school reform is simple. It is not. But I think that this hymn has more to teach us about school reform than the ideas that have guided our efforts since the publication of *A Nation at Risk* (National Commission on Excellence in Education, 1983). This hymn speaks of life and learning in a community of shared aims, reciprocity, and mutual regard. Most of the views that shape modern views of school reform pursuant to *A Nation at Risk* ignore the importance of community, preferring instead to talk about standards, choice, and accountability. Economic goals dominate. In this book I argue that community is the missing element of school reform. More than this, the idea that authentic learning requires community is the core idea of a paradigm of school reform that is an alternative to what we have been attempting for the last 3 decades. The reforms that followed *A Nation at Risk* have largely failed. We cannot continue to tweak them hoping to finally get them to work. As the lyrics at the start of the chapter say, we need to "turn" if we are to "come out right" about school reform.

I am not going to spend much time arguing that the kinds of school reform we have been engaged in since the publication of *A Nation at Risk* have failed. I think this is by now fairly obvious, especially if one judges these reforms by their aspirations. It is more important to try to understand why they failed and what to do about it, and *community* is the key.

We educate our children, and especially our adolescents, in schools that are often not very friendly to their developmental needs. We do not understand the conditions under which children come to value the education adults wish to provide. Schools are often alienating places. If we are to overcome this alienation, we need to think of schools as communities and help our children find a sense of belonging in the schools they attend. Good schools are strong communities. It is the purpose of this book to develop a vision of what it means for schools to be good and strong communities.

This book is also about small schools. The small schools movement is among the most hopeful trends in educational reform. Small schools have the most potential to create places of learning that are strong communities. To realize their potential small schools must be created with a clear view of what a good educational community is.

Schools that are good and strong communities have common purposes—a shared educational project—that define their mission. They provide a common educational experience for their students. They work together to achieve common goods. They are intellectual communities and democratic communities. They are like guilds, congregations, or choirs. In contrast, schools that are not communities tend to see their task as educating their students to be workers and consumers. They seek to develop human capital to enable individual success, productivity, and competitiveness. Their students are viewed as members of the species *homo economicus*. They try to be everything to everyone. They are like banks or shopping malls in that they provide a service but do not require shared purpose among those who use them.

These schools sometimes work well enough for middle class children whose families and communities provide the kinds of social capital that enable success. They are, however, often disasters for urban children who may not come to school with this kind of social capital. These students may find themselves anonymous, lonely, and alienated from the adults in the school, and they may find a sense of belonging in a peer culture that rejects the educational values of the school. They may experience the school as "owned" by a culture not their own and that devalues who they are.

Small schools address alienation by seeking to provide an environment where each student is known to the adults in the school and valued by them. They also aim to be coherent institutions where a vision of a good education is shared by members of the community. This seems a positive way to address the needs of urban populations—and of adolescents generally.

Unhappily, the small schools movement is showing signs of weakness. While most of the research about small schools is encouraging, recent evaluations of attempts to create significant numbers of small schools in urban areas are less encouraging. I will suggest that this may be because the emphasis has been more on downsizing schools than on using small schools as a way to create strong educational communities. Too often the hope has been that if we just create small schools something good will happen. This is a path to failure. Attention needs to be paid to what makes a small school a good educational community. If we create small schools without adequate clarity as to what a good school community is, it is very likely that in a few years the small schools movement will join the long list of failed educational fads. Clarity about community is crucial to success.

These thoughts suggest the story I want to tell here. First, I want to develop a view about what makes a school a good educational community. Second, I want to discuss how the small schools movement fits into this picture of schools as communities. This part of the story will involve an argument as to what we should mean by "small school," one that involves a picture of how school organizations should change and a view about authentic teaching and learning. It will also suggest policies that will help create small schools that are strong communities. Finally, I want to present the resulting conception of small schools that are strong communities as an alternative paradigm for school reform, one that I contrast with two dominant alternatives, standards-based reform and market-oriented choice. Hence the title of the book: *Small Schools and Strong Communities: A Third Way of School Reform.*

Three aphorisms express the central ideas of this book and suggest the concepts that need to be developed:

> Authentic learning is an act of affiliation.
> We are all in this together.
> Alienation is the problem; community is the cure.

These ideas are central to the story I want to tell, which begins by trying to show why community is important for education and ends with a discussion about educational policy and small schools. The introduction in Chapter 1 lays out the themes of the book and explains these three aphorisms in more detail.

In Part I, I focus on the idea that schools should be communities. Chapter 2 shows why community is essential for learning and also why it is hard to achieve. Chapter 3 develops a theory of schools that are communities. Chapters 4 and 5 talk about two forms of community that should characterize good schools: community of practice and democratic community.

In Part II, I focus on characteristics of small schools. Chapter 6 discusses what is meant by the term *small schools* and suggests that if it is going to mean something capable of being a real force for school reform, it must mean more than just having fewer students than large schools. Small schools also need to have certain organizational characteristics and certain ways of seeing teaching and learning: They need coherence of purpose. Chapter 7 describes policies for scaling up good small schools and sustaining them by intentionally creating schools that have the characteristics described in Chapter 6. Chapter 8 takes up the idea that small schools that are strong communities is a distinct paradigm of school reform and discusses in detail how this paradigm differs from standards-based reform and market-oriented choice. Chapter 9 continues the argument of Chapter 8 by applying it to the idea of accountability. Chapter 10 concludes the book with a summary and discusses some caveats and doubts.

There are many fine educators who have put effort into developing successful small schools. I have profited greatly by reading works by educators such as Deborah Meier (2002a, 2002b), Thomas Toch (2003), and Joe Nathan and Karen Febey (2001). These people are persuasive in part because they tell good stories based on their practice and their experience. While I also have a few such stories to tell, this book does not aim to tell stories about good schools. It aims to develop a theory that makes sense of these stories and weaves them together into a narrative about how we should reform American schools.

This book is, however, shaped by stories about successful small schools and by my encounters with small schools and schools that are communities. For example, some years ago I visited a Friends school in the Baltimore area. I talked with various teachers and the principal for the better part of a day about their aspirations and strategies. I was particularly interested in their discussions of Quaker values and about their all-school meeting. When I was leaving, I passed by two students who were talking about an altercation that had just been narrowly avoided. One student said to the other, "I wanted to paste him, but then I thought I should look for the spark of God within." (The actual vocabulary was somewhat more colorful.)

Few of the students or staff in this school were Quakers. Their Quakerism has undergone a secular transformation and there is little that occurred in this school that could not occur in a public school. Yet these people have learned and can speak a language that has Quaker roots, and they have practices that teach this language to newcomers. Probably they do not mean phrases like "the spark of God within" literally or as Quakers understand it. They seem to mean nothing much more than "look for the good in people." Yet they can use this phrase usefully in their interactions, and it helps to shape these interactions in a more communal direction. They seek out the good in others. They seek to create a community that reflects some of the values expressed by the Shaker song at the start of this chapter. They do this in part because they have a shared language that enables this. We cannot see what we cannot say. We cannot do what we cannot conceptualize.

What I learned from this experience has become a part of my view about what creates a community. Community is not just about warm personal relationships. Nor is it simply about shared values. People in schools can like each other and still lack common purpose. Indeed, they can share many values—

individualism, greed, or a desire for good plumbing–and not live in a community. Community is more about a common language that shapes educational purpose, discourse, perception, and personal interactions. People in community can communicate and cooperate because they share a way of thinking and communicating that is rooted in shared commitments. It is these things that make them a community. People in community may not always agree, but they have a common language and share common aspirations. They can communicate and cooperate. And they can trust.

If we are to reform American education, we need to focus less on things like holding educators accountable and how to structure incentives for performance and more on how to create schools where the members of the school community see what they are doing as a kind of mission and have a shared understanding of what this mission is. We need to create schools where kids are known and valued and where they come to share the aspirations of their community for their education and their lives. To do this we need to "turn." If we do not, it is unlikely that things will "come out right."

Small Schools
and
Strong Communities

A THIRD WAY OF SCHOOL REFORM

CHAPTER 1

Introduction

Community, Small Schools, and School Reform

We need to surround kids with adults who know and care for our children, who have opinions and are accustomed to expressing them publicly, and who know how to reach reasonable collective decisions in the face of disagreement. That means increasing local decision making, and simultaneously decreasing the size and bureaucratic complexity of schools.
–Deborah Meier, *Will Standards Save Public Education?*, p. 20

In the preface I suggested three aphorisms that I believe capture the essential ideas of this book. They bear repeating:

Authentic learning is an act of affiliation.
We are all in this together.
Alienation is the problem: community is the cure.

Below I explore their meaning in more detail.

AUTHENTIC LEARNING AND COMMUNITY

Good schools need to be communities. They need to be communities because there is an intimate connection between authentic learning and belonging. They need to be communities because good education is more likely to occur when we approach teaching and learning with a sense that we are all in this together. They need to be communities because our children are often alienated from the education we wish to provide, and community is the cure for alienation.

Let's consider these three aphorisms. The first says two things. It says that when we feel ourselves to be members of a community we are likely also to find it important to master those things that are central to the goals and shared understandings of that community. We affirm our membership through learning those things our community cares about. And it says that when we learn something authentically, we become members of a community. We create our membership by internalizing the values, shared understandings, beliefs, and skills that are distinct to the community.

When people learn the kinds of things taught in schools, they become members of communities of practitioners whose activities, conversations, and arguments sustain human social activities that I will call (following Alasdair MacIntyre, 1981) *practices*. When we learn authentically, we affiliate with communities of practice. We become artists, or scientists, or crafts persons. We are shaped by the values, ideas, and activities of these communities of practice. Learning involves affiliation. Affiliation is transformative. Affiliation makes us human and humane. Music, mathematics, physics, art, farming, woodworking, tennis, and football are among the practices that make us human and humane.

The second aphorism concerns a different form of community: democratic community. A *democratic community* is one where all are valued equally regardless of differences such as religion, gender, ethnicity, or capacity. It is a community in which some goods, common goods, are pursued together and in which people see themselves as succeeding together. It is a community where the views of all are fairly considered.

These two types of community, community of practice and democratic community, are the essential forms of community that should be pursued in schools–all schools.

The third aphorism is about school reform. A persistent theme of educators is that many of their students are not much interested in learning what adults want to teach them. How to get them engaged is a constant topic of discussion. Yet modern pictures of school reform do not adequately address student disengagement. They do not do this because they do not understand that genuine learning is an act of affiliation that requires strong communities and educational practices that successfully connect students to these communities. Indeed most visions of school reform undercut community.

They do this because they have a picture of education that is too individualistic and instrumental. When they think about getting students engaged they tend to think about this by asking how to create incentives for student performance or how the curriculum can be made more interesting. Recent proposals have added outright bribery to the list of suggestions.

While these strategies have a place, they miss the centrality of alienation and disengagement as educational problems, and they miss the importance of community as the central cure for them. The real cure for disengagement is to create communities of common purpose for students so that they come to share the goals we have for them. Hence my third aphorism: Alienation is the problem; community is the cure.

Creating small schools can help create schools that are communities, but good educational communities do not automatically happen when schools have fewer students. We must take thought to create schools that have the kinds of characteristics suggested by Deborah Meier in the chapter epigraph above.

Creating community is hard. There are numerous features of our society and deeply rooted ideological commitments of our culture that make community hard. The pervasive anti-intellectualism of our culture (Jacoby, 2008) makes good educational community hard. The fragmentation of social life into many weak and partial associations makes community hard. Our overly bureaucratic, centralized, and incoherent educational system makes school community hard.

If we are to have schools that are good and strong communities and if the small schools movement is to succeed in helping to reform American education, we will need a good deal more clarity than we now have about what a good school community is and about how to create community in public schools. Community is a complex idea. Policies to achieve community in schools are fraught with difficulties. We cannot just muddle through about this.

A school not far from where this paragraph is being written has a banner hanging in front that proclaims it to be a community of caring. I am not sure what this banner means. From a few conversations with teachers, they are not sure either. The sign conveys a warm, fuzzy feeling, but provides no real guide to action or policy. *Community* is an honorific, but vague, term. Much depends on what is meant by it.

Communities are constituted by something more than strong affective ties. They are created by something shared, by the common understandings, norms, and experiences of their members. Thus it matters what understandings, norms, and experiences are shared.

In creating community in schools we need to find a balance between conceptions of community that are too "thin" and too "thick." If we have a conception of community that is too thin—that fails to bind people together by values and norms that involve a substantive and praiseworthy conception of a good education—we may reduce the idea of community to something about the "personalization" of education or about creating caring relations between adults and kids.

Personalization and caring are good things, and we do not have enough of them, but they will not, by themselves, sustain a vision of a good educational community. If personalization and care are all that energize the small schools movement, that movement will not serve to provide a new paradigm of school reform. It will become just another "technique" in implementing standards-based reform. Community requires more. Strong communities require shared understandings, norms, and experiences. They need what I call a *shared educational project*–a shared and public conception of what they are about and how they will achieve it.

If, however, our conception of community is too thick, if we are inflexibly devoted to some vision of the One Truth or the One Right Way, we run the risk of creating communities that are parochial or oppressive (Peshkin, 1986). As Coleman and Hoffer (1987) have noted, schools have two roles that can conflict. They can be seen as extensions of the home, church, and the local community and function as instruments to convey the values that predominate in these places. They can also be seen as windows on the larger world and instruments to overcome parochial values and develop a capacity for critical thinking.

My vision of community respects both roles, but gives pride of place to the second. Good school communities are liberating. Bad communities suffocate cognitive growth and limit vision and opportunity. They have a dark side (Noddings, 1996). They can be intolerant of those who are not members. In arguing for schools that are communities, I do not wish to legitimate schools that are parochial or oppressive. At the same time, good communities must be rooted somehow; otherwise, instead of promoting growth and vision, they will create students who are anomic and rootless. Educational communities need to be thick enough to do their jobs, but not so thick as to become total communities.

The idea that schools should be communities contains a vision of school reform whose core assumptions can be distinguished from the core assumptions of other paradigms of school reform. Effective school reform is not primarily about standards or accountability or performance incentives. It is about belonging and about initiating students into communities that create and sustain excellence in practices. And it is about creating democratic communities that help create good citizens and good neighbors. It is about being more concerned with the kinds of learning that enrich lives and create democratic social relationships than with the development of human capital, although we must be concerned with that as well.

SCHOOL REFORM: OLD PARADIGMS IN OLDER BOTTLES?

We need a new vision of school reform because our reform efforts since *A Nation at Risk* (National Commission on Excellence in Education, 1983) have largely failed, and they have exhausted their resources for renewal. If one dates current reform efforts from *A Nation at Risk*, we are midway into the 3rd decade of a series of reforms that have emphasized increased rigor, statewide or national standards, a more academic curriculum, expanded accountability, and ever more testing. We have gone through several waves of reform, each substantially motivated by the failure of its predecessor. It is becoming increasingly clear that we have gotten little from all of this reforming.

Even if here and there we have made modest gains in test scores, the gains we have made fall far short of the aspirations of reformers, and it is often unclear whether they are attributable to current reform efforts. Goals 2000 (1994), the signature reform of the Clinton administration, aspired for the United States to be first in the world in math and science by 2000. We are not. Little has changed in our international standing since 1993. We were told that 90% of our students would graduate; only about 75% do.

One indicator is particularly salient. National Assessment of Educational Progress (NAEP) scale scores in reading since 1972 (NAEP, 2004), show modest gains for 9-year-olds, and even more modest gains for 13-year-olds. Results for 17-year-olds are, however, basically flat. High school students test no better now than they did in 1972. Math scores tell essentially the same story. There are modest gains for younger students, but trivial gains for 17-year-olds. The math scores may be more telling about the extent to which reform has failed since math is generally viewed as more responsive to instruction than is reading. These numbers suggest that gains in achievement are quite modest at all levels of schooling and are often given back in high school.

A second set of statistics similarly shows little improvement. The National Center for Educational Statistics (2000) claims that "despite the increased importance of a high school education for entry to postsecondary education and the labor market, the high school completion rate has shown limited gains over the last three decades and has been stable throughout the 1990s" (p. 23). While completion rates have edged up slightly in this decade, they are alarmingly low in many urban areas and for poor and minority students (NCES, 2007).

These facts are broadly conceded. Yet many want to respond to them by expanding No Child Left Behind (NCES, 2002) accountability to the high school level and into more subjects, even though few now believe that NCLB has been effective. It appears that the escalating requirements of annual yearly progress (AYP) benchmarks will soon lead to most schools being judged to be failing schools. It seems very unlikely that all, or even most, students will be proficient by 2014. Many believe that because NCLB distorts the curriculum and provides perverse incentives it has done real harm to our schools (Nichols and Berliner, 2007a, 2007b; Rothstein, Jacobson, & Wilder, 2008).

No Child Left Behind seems to survive because we cannot agree on how to fix it and do not see viable alternatives to it. But extending its strategies seems a little like trying to turn leeching into an effective medical practice by using more leeches. Before we do this, perhaps the ineffectiveness of more than 3 decades of educational reform should cause us to reflect more carefully on the core assumptions that drive our views of school reform.

What are the assumptions of current paradigms of school reform? One assumption is that standards are central to school reform. A *standard* is an answer to the question, "What do we want students to know and to be able to do?" Standards get published in booklets and can be used to guide curriculum development and test construction. Having high standards is supposed to make our education more rigorous.

Standards are valued for a number of reasons. First, they are supposed to be important in creating a coherent educational system. When we have standards, we can align teacher training, curriculum, tests, and other components of the educational system so that the parts work together.

A second reason to have standards is that we need to hold educators accountable. We do this by developing tests aligned with our standards and using them to create achievement benchmarks that educators are expected to meet. And we attach rewards and penalties to these benchmarks.

A third argument for standards is that they, and the tests that measure whether we have met them, are important if we are to provide information to the "consumers" of education—parents and community members. Standards enable competent choice or competent policy deliberations, or, at least, the public shaming of educators who fail in their tasks.

A final reason to have standards is to ensure that the kind of education offered in the best schools is offered everywhere.

This picture of school reform has some crucial features we should note. One is that we can effectively run a complex educational system from the center. We must believe that education is the kind of thing that can be effectively managed by a centralized governmental bureaucracy. Often people seeking to justify reforms that emphasize accountability to a state-imposed management system point to how successful corporations are run as their model. Their opponents suggest that a better analogy might be the dysfunction of planned economies.

A second feature of this picture is its tendency to standardize curricular content. This standardization is sometimes motivated by a belief that the same curriculum is best for every child, but it is more often pursued because it is a condition of an educational system and of accountability. We cannot hold teachers accountable for meeting test-based benchmarks if different schools have different curricula. The standards movement leads to curricular content that is as much influenced by bureaucratic needs as by the needs of children. There is no vision of the content of good education that motivates it.

A third feature is the conviction that behavior is largely motivated by incentives. No Child Left Behind is not merely a means to discover what kids have learned. It rewards their schools for their success and penalizes their failure.

High-stakes tests similarly employ rewards and penalties to motivate students. Indeed, some have argued that a main reason why students are disengaged is that nothing depends on their educational success, and that we should make jobs or access to further education depend on educational attainment (Bishop, 1989). To do that we must have standards and benchmarks, and we must test to see if we have met them. Such views emphasize the instrumental value of learning over the capacity of education to enrich our lives.

Standards-based reform, however, is not the only model of reform on the contemporary table. Its main alternative has been "choice." In the policy arena, advocacy for choice schemes such as vouchers and charter schools has often been rooted in a strong belief in markets and market competition. Moreover, choice advocates are suspicious of whether government bureaucracies can effectively and efficiently regulate a large and complex educational system.

Nevertheless, choice has much in common with standards-based reform. It places strong emphasis on incentives, although its advocates believe that these incentives are more effectively generated by markets than by government bureaucracies. Many choice advocates continue to value standards and testing. Often they view this as a means to providing consumer information, but they accept the standardization that it implies.

These two models of school reform are rooted in conflicting views of the role of government and markets in providing services. The macro debate in American politics has been the debate between those who believe in the capacity of government to act purposefully and effectively to better the lives of Americans and those who argue for the importance of markets and seek a diminished role for government—state versus market, Max Weber (Camic et al., 2005) versus Adam Smith (1976). If we think that these are the major options, we will have difficulty escaping the blinders that characterize our debates about educational policy.

The assumptions underlying modern school-reform movements are significantly anticommunity and seem likely to increase the alienation of students and teachers. They tend to erode authentic teaching because authentic learning is difficult to capture in standards and tests and because the modern accountability movement tends to substitute testing for the appraisal of competent judges. They even rob us of the language we need to discuss authentic learning by defining notions such as excellence and rigor in term of test-based benchmarks instead of high-quality performance.

They also erode community by centralizing authority and taking judgment out of the hands of teachers and school leaders. Teachers are viewed more as functionaries in a bureaucratic system than as professionals committed to professional standards and motivated by the welfare of their students. It becomes difficult to see schools as autonomous or as local democratic communities.

Student alienation is increased by standardization. According to a bygone presidential report on education (Coleman, 1974), students are increasingly faced with only one way to grow up. Their individual capacities or projects matter little. Subsequent reforms have made this worse.

Finally, modern reform efforts erode community because they aim largely at human capital formation—individual success and collective productivity. They lack a sense that education can enrich lives as well as make us rich. They have no sense of creating citizens who care for the common good. And they have no sense of cooperation to achieve shared ends. They have reduced good education to raising test scores in the belief that this will secure prosperity. In policy circles the resulting alienation of students and teachers goes without much notice.

We thus face a dilemma. Strong communities are essential to good education. They are required to address the core problem of alienation. But thought about school reform is dominated by a state versus market debate, and questions about how we can create strong communities are not on the table. They do not fit the prevailing paradigms.

COMMUNITY AND SMALL SCHOOLS: A WAY FORWARD?

The idea that schools should be communities provides us with an alternative picture of school reform to the ones expressed by the state versus market debate. But, if we do not have a coherent and robust view of what it means for schools to be communities, the idea is likely to be gutted so as to domesticate it to fit with other models with more visibility and clout. Making schools into communities will become just another strategy in a test-driven system. We cannot view the idea that schools should be communities as simply complementary to standards-based reform or to choice. The core assumptions of these views are different from and inconsistent with the idea that schools should be communities.

Those who advocate for small schools often note that one reason they work is that they are communities. Mary Anne Raywid and Gil Schmerler (2003) comment on the dilemma small schools face: "Small schools . . . are intended to do more than just replicate the status quo on a smaller scale. The successful ones involve changes in curricular organization, instructional strategy, the organization of teachers' work, school culture, school and student assessment, and more" (p. x). Many of the changes Raywid and Schmerler advocate are precisely the things that help make small schools more communal. But these new ways of doing things challenge conventional wisdom not only about education but about how schools are operated and how they are reformed.

If we do not see this, and if we are not prepared to advocate for small schools that are also strong communities, we will reduce the idea that schools should be communities to an empty platitude, and we will make small schools simply downsized versions of big schools. We will talk about community, and perhaps we will put up banners announcing we are communities of caring, but we will change nothing of importance, and we will continue pursuing the same alienating views of school reform and accountability that have failed us since the modern school-reform era began with *A Nation at Risk*.

We need to root a discussion of community and of small schools in a larger social and historical context. Schools are expressions of their societies. Our society in turn is an expression of historical and political forces. We are democratic and capitalist. Most of us are urbanites. We are the product of a centuries-long social evolution that has transformed western societies and created the conditions of modern life. Few of us now live in small villages and towns where we know everyone we meet, where we work and play with the same people, where we worship in the same church and share the same religion, and where our actions are governed by shared understandings and a shared culture. We now live in a society where we interact in many different weak associations with people who are often strangers and who do not share our commitments and culture. The norms we follow often differ from where we work to where we play to where we worship. Our interactions are often anonymous, negotiated, contractual, and codified. Compliance substitutes for trust.

This world has given us much. It has made many people in the developed world rich by historical standards. It has given us liberal democracy which, whatever one thinks of its recent manifestations, is surely an improvement over feudalism and monarchy. Our view of community cannot look backward to a simpler age. In our search for community we cannot succumb to what philosopher Richard Rorty (1981) has called "terminal wistfulness."

Yet modernity has had a cost. It has made many people rootless, anomic, and lonely. It has weakened relationships and community. We now live in many partial communities most of which have a weak hold on us. Attachments to place are weak. People change jobs and locations for modest financial gain. We do not know our neighbors well. We view most of our relationships as temporary. Children move away. Friends drift apart. Divorce rates are high, and those who stay married sometimes live largely separate lives. We join clubs or civic groups and leave them easily. Religious people change congregations and religions frequently. They shop for faith, and they view their place of worship as a means to their own satisfaction more than as a source of truths that make claims on them.

The weakness of attachments in the larger society infects schools. Students are not likely to know their teachers or other students in nonschool contexts. Large schools often begin as and remain a world of strangers. Belonging is sought more in subgroups than as a member of a whole school community. Youth culture dominates moral development. Teachers are fragmented into departmental groups with different cultures and different aspirations. Trust is absent. Behavior is shaped more by regulation than by the moral authority of adults.

Schools that merely reflect modernity are likely to be cafeterias of cultural goods (Sizer, 1984) where students have much freedom of choice but little guidance as to how wise choices are made and what is worthwhile. In trying to serve diverse populations, modern schools tend to privatize the goals they serve, present a curriculum that lacks coherence, and cope with cultural diversity by affirming tolerance and equality while standing for nothing else of educational substance. They seek to equip students to pursue self-chosen lives by providing knowledge and skills that are economically valuable, but they convey little about how to lead a good life and little about what is just or worthwhile. The people they serve are viewed as members of the species *homo economicus*. Many schools have a tacit ethic: Get an education to get a job to get money to get stuff. They teach "possessive individualism." Such schools are more like banks or shopping malls than communities.

In short, under modernity, communities are weakened in their capacity to educate. Schools reflect this weakness. This is more of a problem than most educational theorists have grasped. A vision of school reform needs to take alienation and disengagement as central problems and seek to restore the role of adults and healthy adult communities in the lives of children.

Small schools offer the potential of some amelioration of the conditions that alienate and disengage students. Their smallness creates conditions under which relationships can be stronger. They are not communities in virtue of their smallness, but smallness makes community easier.

The small schools movement has its roots in two very different kinds of institutions. One source is rural schools, schools that are small in virtue of population demographics. Students, parents, and teachers already know one another. The school is a center of community activity. Often these schools struggle to be comprehensive schools. They are often good schools both because they are small and because they are rooted in local community. At the same time they are not representative of the kinds of schools that dominate American education.

A second type of small school is the type that is being created in many urban areas: New York, Chicago, Philadelphia, and Cincinnati, to name a few. These schools often have themed curricula and seek to avoid being comprehensive schools. Those who inhabit them are often strangers when they walk through the doors. Indeed, because small schools are often schools of choice and do not recruit their students from one neighborhood this may be more likely in small schools than in other urban schools. Such schools try to create community from an aggregation of strangers by being distinctive and by having clear and transparent purposes that are shared by staff, parents, and students.

It is a mistake to think that these different types of schools are instances of the same thing. If we see them as the same we do so because we look only at size and ignore what makes them distinctive. But they are communities of quite different types. Small rural schools tend to be communities of place. Small urban schools are communities of purpose. Both forms of community are fine, but they are different. We should not assume that they work in the same way. Communities of place build on familiarity, local roots, and attachment to a place. Communities of purpose must create cohesion among strangers. They begin with a coherent and shared mission.

I will emphasize the second type of small school, for it is schools of this sort that have the potential to make a major contribution to school reform. This contribution, however, is only going to be made if small schools are viewed as communities of shared purpose. If we proceed on the assumption that all there is to the idea of a small school is scale and personalization, these schools will fail to shed the anticommunal practices that undermine good education.

Schools need to create two forms of community. First, they need to be intellectual communities. They should provide an education that is humane and humanistic in its character—an education more concerned with human flourishing than human capital. The idea that schools should be intellectual communities means that there are certain norms that should pervade every school. Ideas count. Inquiry is important. Good schools teach students how to use their minds. They view what they teach as practices and emphasize authentic teaching. They see subjects as human activities - things people do together. When students learn a subject, they are initiated into a community of practice.

The emphasis on practices suggests that schools need a focused and robust vision of the educational commitments that should infuse their curriculum. We need to shed the idea of the comprehensive school if that means having schools that try to be everything to everyone rather than schools that include everyone. Schools should create a common experience for their students and in most cases should emphasize a particular theme or curricular focus. They should be schools of the arts, or of ecology, or of social justice, or of equine science. But more important, they should emphasize the goods that are internal to practices—how these practices enrich us more than how they make us rich. This requires a distinctive form of teaching, authentic teaching, teaching that is transformative.

Second, every school should also be a democratic community. Some schools, the Friends Schools for example, have all-school meetings where everyone can participate in discussing the issues of the day. I think this is commendable, but I do not think it is required. What is required is a strong sense of the dignity and worth of each member of the school community, a strong commitment to the common good, and a strong desire to include everyone because everyone is valuable. Democratic communities are committed to the idea of WITT–"We're in this together" (Bernstein, 2006). Most modern American schools are more committed to YOYO–"You're on your own." Often the test of a democratic community is how the weakest and neediest members are treated. Democratic communities are inclusive and participatory.

These two conceptions of community reinforce each other. If we teach our students to value mathematics and science because success in these subjects is the key to getting into a good college and eventually into a lucrative career, we also teach them that they are in competition with each other for scarce rewards. If, however, we teach them to love mathematics and science (or craft or sport) because they enable us to understand and better appreciate the world and because mastery improves our minds and our souls, we focus on these things in a way that deemphasizes competition and emphasizes the shared pursuit of common goals and common goods. In this second case, it is easier to believe that we really are all in this together. Good communities are like sports teams or music groups. People succeed as a collectivity.

Of course competition for places in higher education and desirable careers is a fact of life. It is not created by schools and cannot be repealed by them. Schools will inevitably function to distribute various scarce social goods. Creating schools that are communities will not change this. The difference is a matter of emphasis. Do we approach subjects primarily as instruments to careers, or do we approach subjects more broadly as things that can enrich our lives? If the "body language" of our schools teaches, "Get schooling to get jobs to get money to get stuff," we should not expect them to be communities. If we want to create community, we need to emphasize learning because it enriches our lives.

This picture of schools as communities requires the proper material conditions and the proper policies. It is not altogether essential that communities be small, but smallness makes creating community easier. It helps to make adults more important in the lives of kids. It creates the social capital that enables learning. It enables communication, informal organizations, collegiality, and trust.

Similarly we need the right policies. Schools that are communities need considerable autonomy if they are to pursue a distinctive course. They need to be free to develop their own conception of a good education and to recruit teachers and students who share their vision. And they need to be schools of choice, not because competition leads to efficiency, but because free association–the ability to cooperate in a common project with the like-minded–is important to creating coherent communities.

We also need a different view of motivation and of accountability. Modern pictures of school reform have emphasized incentives linked to test-defined benchmarks. We need a view that emphasizes collegiality, professionalism, and the intrinsic value of learning. And we need a view of governance that places more emphasis on local decision making and community participation and less on accountability to a governmental bureaucracy.

Ultimately, we need a new vision of school reform that takes community seriously, and we need to hold schools accountable for creating good educational communities.

I find the idea that schools should be communities a hopeful one, and I find the small schools movement to be a promising way forward. This much might have been said of many movements that failed. Having a good idea is one thing; getting it to work in complex bureaucratic systems is another. Change is hard; changes that require people to think differently are harder. New schools are created by human beings. Human beings are fallible and self-interested. They will screw up. Some ventures will fail. All will require a shakedown cruise to get the bugs out—and there will be a lot of bugs. Patience is required. Here, clarity of aspiration is not everything, but it is essential.

We should not, however, see small schools that are strong communities as a silver bullet. I know of no evidence that suggests that any school reform alone can eliminate achievement gaps or dramatically improve the education of children in high-poverty communities. The roots of inequality and educational mediocrity lie beyond the schoolhouse door. No society that tolerates as much poverty as ours does or devalues intellectual accomplishment as much as ours does should expect schools to magically succeed. When we have a culture that tolerates massive inequality, disvalues the poor, is dominated by consumerism, and is often anti-intellectual, good school communities must sometimes be like monasteries. They are in, but not of, their local communities. They protect people from the local community and preserve what is of value against an oppositional cultural tide. This is, of course, overstated. At the same time, the communities in which many young people are raised are not always assets to good education. We must sometimes hope that schools can make a difference in an unsupportive environment. We can hope and aspire, but let us not be naive.

Dramatic improvement in our schools is only likely as part of a broader attack on poverty. Poor children need stable housing, good health care, employed parents, and good preschools (Berliner, 2006; Rothstein, 2002, 2004).

While the small schools movement linked to the idea that schools should be communities may seem a schools-only approach, we can also see it as the expression of a broader and more egalitarian agenda. The democratic element in a suitable theory of school community can help restore some of the focus on equality. And it does this in a way that goes beyond thinking of educational equality in terms of achievement gaps to include a concept motivated by the ideal of equal citizenship, the pursuit of common goods, and full inclusion. It affirms WITT over YOYO.

A central theme in my argument is that the quality of community counts. This theme is certainly about schools, but it has obvious application beyond schools. If we want kids to do well in schools, we need to emphasize the creation of quality communities that nourish their growth beyond the walls of the school. We cannot expect schools to fully overcome the consequences of impoverished or morally toxic environments (Gabarino, 1995) outside of the school. If we are serious about equality, a comprehensive approach that emphasizes creating quality communities is required.

Small schools that are strong communities will not alleviate poverty and its consequences for the education of poor children. Nor will they enable schools to dramatically increase achievement in the face of daunting obstacles rooted in poverty. They may, however, play a role in creating a society in which it is thought that we are all in this together. Such a consciousness is required if we are to address poverty. And along the way it may help to create schools in which the quality of life of students in our urban schools is valued and improved and where they learn more than would otherwise have been the case. These things are not everything. But they are not nothing either.

Small schools that aspire to be communities can be a source of hope. They can create supportive educational communities for students whose communities beyond the walls are not nurturing or educative. With work and dedication and coherence, they can make a real difference in the lives of young people. But let us not see them as silver bullets or as a panacea for the ills of a society that too often lacks supportive environments for its young. No vision of school reform should serve as a substitute for the creation of a more democratic and egalitarian society.

Part I

EDUCATION
and
COMMUNITY

CHAPTER 2

Learning, Belonging, and School Reform

Why Community Is Necessary and Why Community Is Hard

Upon this gifted age, in its dark hour,
Falls from the sky a meteoric shower
Of facts . . . they lie unquestioned, uncombined.
Wisdom enough to leech us of our ill
Is daily spun; but there exists no loom
To weave it into fabric . . .
–Edna St. Vincent Millay, "Upon this age, that never speaks its mind"

WHY COMMUNITY IS NECESSARY

We live in an information-rich age. As Edna St. Vincent Milay's poem suggests, facts rain down on us relentlessly. How are we to make sense of them? Making sense of things is part of an education that aims to enrich us more than make us rich. Good education provides the loom with which such a fabric is woven.

If we are to help students weave a fabric for their lives, we need to emphasize the humanistic potential of their education. The subjects schools teach– mathematics, art, science, music, history, language–contain material from which a fabric can be woven. ― *for a specific student (racy, curet.)*

If we are to help students weave a fabric, we also need to teach them properly. We need what I call "authentic teaching and learning." We need an education that shows students how ideas orient and enrich. We need to show the values and the norms that are part of these subjects. We need to teach subjects in ways that are transformative, not just economically functional. We need to remember the connection between learning and belonging.

Authentic teaching is teaching that faithfully represents the nature of the sub-

17

ject being taught. The authentic teaching of writing, for example, shows concern for the beauty and expressiveness of language, not just grammar, spelling, and punctuation. It cares for persuasive argument, not just the organization of topics. It gives students experience in doing research and also in writing poetry. It recognizes the social character of the practice of writing by representing the practices of a community to a new generation of potential members. It makes *authentic learning* an act of affiliation with a community. The defining characteristic of authentic teaching is that social practices are represented faithfully and accurately. Student learning points toward authentic performances, not just high test scores.

Authentic teaching does not reduce subjects to lists of facts, theories, and skills. When we learn something authentically, we internalize norms, ideas, and skills that were developed by and are maintained by the interactions of the members of various communities. We develop excellences that help us realize the aims of these communities. Academic subjects, art and music, craft and sport, and occupations are not just static bodies of facts, theories, and skills. They are human activities–practices–and their concepts, norms, theories, and skills are created and maintained by human communities. There is no physics without a community of physicists, no art without a community of artists. The things that we teach and students sometimes learn in schools are things people do in communities.

People learn by interacting with communities. This is how we learn to speak, how we learn our religious convictions, how we learn to play tennis, and how we learn mathematics. We internalize what others have produced and what others already possess. When we do this we are transformed. We are able to experience and appreciate the world in new ways–ways invented by others and sustained by communities. When we learn to play tennis, not only can we hit balls over nets, we can also see a serve and volley and appreciate a well-struck backhand.

As we learn, we become more like those others who have already been transformed by learning what we are now learning. We come to see ourselves in them, and they come to see themselves in us. We become Spanish speakers, musicians, Catholics, chess players, mathematicians, footballers, and carpenters. We learn through affiliation, and we affiliate through learning. If we do not learn by interacting with and internalizing the achievements of communities, what we learn is static and dead, not a human activity and not authentic learning.

The context for authentic teaching and learning is a relationship between someone who is accomplished in what is being taught and someone who is not. It involves showing as much as telling. And it involves providing feedback on current performance, something that requires expert judgment. Students do things under the watchful eye of someone who knows how these things are done. As the Coalition of Essential Schools (2006) suggests, good teachers are like coaches, and students are like workers, not workers in the sense of employees, but workers in the sense that what they do is like what real practitioners of the practice do. They are more like apprentices than students.

Good teachers are both masters and emissaries. They represent the achievements of their communities to the next generation. They seek to show the next generation the worth of their practices so that students internalize not only facts and skills, but ways of seeing and valuing, feeling and appreciating. Good teachers seek new members of their communities. They do this by exemplifying what is worthy in their craft before their students.

To learn is to come to belong. When we internalize the norms, ideas, theories, and skills of a community, we are shaped by these things so that we become members of the community on whose interactions these norms, ideas, theories, and skills depend. This is true of language communities, religious communities, occupational communities, and intellectual communities. Genuine learning is an act of affiliation.

Authentic learning involves what I call "normation" (Green, 1999)—a concept that I develop more rigorously in the next chapter. *Normation* concerns the internalization of the norms and the goods that are internal to and constitutive of practices. *Norms* are standards of excellence and of competence. They tell us what counts as doing something well and what counts as a mistake, what is elegant and what is careless, what is good and what is mediocre, what is well played and what is lucky. People who have learned to write well have acquired more than skills. They have learned what counts as beauty or persuasiveness. They have learned to feel dissatisfied when their writing is awkward or wordy and accomplished when it is polished. Norms thus both define excellence and elicit feelings.

Norms are also perceptual categories. When we have internalized the norms of a particular practice, we can see things we were not able to see before. We are better able to experience beauty, grace, or elegance. Norms express and exhibit values. To internalize a norm is to know what a practice considers good and to appreciate this goodness when it is present. When we have learned to write well, we can see good writing, and we can have those emotions that good writing can inspire.

Thus authentic learning is transformative of perception and motivation. When we have internalized the norms of a given practice, we not only see the world in different ways, but we come to feel differently about it. When we have internalized the norms of a sport, for example, we not only know what counts as playing well, but we come to care about good play. Performing or experiencing a well-executed squeeze bunt or jump shot becomes a kind of aesthetic experience.

This transformative power of internalizing the norms internal to practices is why an emphasis on authentic learning is important to overcoming alienation and disengagement. As we learn something authentically, our motives for doing it change. We come to care about the goods that excellent performance helps us realize, and we enjoy engaging in the practice. Think of learning to play the piano. At the outset people are likely to experience practicing as drudgery. They struggle with elementary skills. They play badly and produce noise. They experience frustration and have to be kept at it. But as they learn to play well they come to appreciate the music they produce and the music produced by others more. People enjoy their own competence, and they enjoy its product, good music.

This kind of learning requires community. It requires a group of people who tend a practice, care about it, refine it, and help initiate new members into it. Schools that successfully engage in authentic teaching help create and extend communities of practice by sharing the practice. Students who are initiated into a community of practice not only achieve mastery of some valued human activity, but they come to share the values of its competent practitioners. They stick to the task of learning, in part, because others whom they trust show them that the practice is valued.

Another type of community that is central to good education is democratic community. Democratic community, like community of practice, is a complex notion, but among its essential elements is WITT ("We're in this together"), a kind of solidarity rooted in equality and in respect for the dignity and worth of all. Creation of democratic community also involves normation. Indeed, democracy is a kind of practice with its own goods and norms (Stout, 2004). Authentic instruction in democracy transforms people into citizens who are members of democratic communities and who experience democratic community as a good in their lives.

The two core aspirations of a theory of school community are (1) to create communities of practice that enrich young lives by encouraging their mastery of practices that human beings have created and found enriching and (2) to create democratic communities that transmit the virtues and values of citizenship.

The failure to learn is often a failure of community. Learning fails when the community that sustains a given practice is no longer able to attract and apprentice new members. Authentic learning depends on trust. When community is weak, trust is difficult to establish, and the relations between the accomplished practitioner and novices are ruptured. Normation fails.

We can view much of the failure of contemporary schooling as a failure of effective intergenerational communication, a failure of community. Students may have to attend school, but they do not have to attend to or care about what adults want to teach. Often they do not. They are disengaged. We have not gained their trust or their attention sufficiently so that they see what adults value as a potential source of value for them. In this sense, they are alienated

what if it's not desd for them

from the education adults seek to provide. They complain that their studies are boring or irrelevant. Teachers, in turn, complain that their students must be constantly entertained and that they regularly try to bargain down the effort expected of them. This is especially true of students in urban areas who drop out of school in unacceptably large numbers. And it is especially true in secondary schools. — NO

I doubt that the cure for student disengagement is to be sought simply in more engaging teaching. Instead, we should view the problem of disengagement as an expression of alienation or anomie that is more deeply rooted. Putting the matter this way is intended to lead us to look for cultural or structural roots of disengagement rather than to look at it merely as a deficiency of our pedagogy. Authentic teaching requires certain social conditions if it is to succeed. It requires communities that are able to effectively endorse worthwhile practices and their norms, namely, strong communities. What is a healthy culture?

In healthy cultures children want to learn what adults have to teach because they wish to become adults in good standing and members of the adult community. This is how they gain status and respect. When adults wish to teach them something, they trust the adults that what they are asked to learn will contribute to the enrichment of their lives and the achievement of adult status. They want to learn because they trust and because they want to be members of the adult communities represented by their caregivers. If students are disengaged, it is because they do not see what is taught in schools either as a potential source of enrichment or as important to becoming a respected adult member of their community. These failures are failures of intergenerational communication and of community.

One is alienated when one must comply with the expectations of an institution whose purposes one does not share. Many students see the education adults wish to provide them as unrelated to their current lives or as related only in virtue of the arbitrary decisions of adults. Some students see the education adults wish to provide as rooted in a culture that is not theirs. They do not see the education that adults offer as a potential source of enrichment or as a path to becoming a respected member of their community. And it is hard to be engaged with algebra when there are cell phones, Facebook, parties, beer, and MTV. If schools cannot convey to students that what they offer is valuable, if they cannot create trust, then students will see their schools as a force arrayed against them. Alienation is a sign that educational communities are not strong enough to do the work of normation.

People are anomic when they lack moral and valuational standards that are sufficient to guide action. To be anomic is to lack purpose or direction. People are anomic when social norms are unclear or confused or when they have failed to internalize norms adequate to provide purpose and direction in life. Anomic people are easily moved by the moment or by the crowd. They

become anomic when the communities available to them are too weak to succeed in transmitting norms.

Given that student disengagement rooted in alienation and anomie is a
core problem to be solved by modern educational systems, it is surprising how
rarely it is seen as the focus of school reform efforts. Modern proposals for
school reform emphasize standards, accountability, and choice. They want to
improve teacher quality and create better curricula. They are about systems,
resources, training, and incentives. Educators recognize the disengagement of
their students, but educational policy is rarely directed toward overcoming it.

I believe that student disengagement, alienation, and anomie are core problems to be dealt with by educational reform movements. Moreover, I claim
that when we focus on disengagement and alienation we get a different picture
of how schools should be reformed, one that is sufficiently at odds with other
views of school reform that we can view it as a distinct paradigm. Alienation is
the problem; community is the solution.

This means that when we want to reform schools the first thing we need to
do is try to understand and create the social conditions under which authentic teaching can succeed and under which learning is not alienated. We need
to understand how we can create strong and good educational communities.
To be sure, this is not all we need to do, but it is the main thing. Authentic
learning is an act of affiliation. A corollary: The failure to learn is a failure of
community.

WHY COMMUNITY IS HARD

There are many forces in our culture that erode community and make the creation of school communities difficult. One of the persistent themes in sociology
for more than a century has been the decline of community under conditions
of modernity. Traditional societies give us communities where, to quote Tevye
in *Fiddler on the Roof,* "Everyone knows who he is and what God expects him
to do." People are united by close and intimate contacts and shared understandings. In "thick" communities we work, play, and worship with the same
people. There are few rules, but many shared norms, norms that define identity
and claim allegiance.

Modernity has greatly weakened such communities. We now live our lives
in many partial communities. We work in one place with one group of people.
We play with others in other places. We worship and we learn in still other
places and with still other people. We are associated in clubs, banks, and bars.
All of these groups and places have different norms. We may often feel as
though we are different people in different places when we have internalized
these varied norms. We have fleeting contacts with many people in many con-

texts. Few of these associations dominate our identity. To a degree, we can choose who we are by choosing our communities. These communities and their associated identities are easily shed; so are our places, jobs, and even our families.

Among the consequences of modern life are loneliness, alienation, and ano-mie. We have many associates, but few close friends; we often experience our institutional lives as dominated by alien forces arrayed against us; we have many choices, but few guidelines for making them. We are inclined to choose our communities merely because they "fit" us or provide satisfaction at the mo-ment rather than because their commitments are true or their values genuinely worthwhile and enduring. Many religious groups no longer proclaim truths or offer salvation as much as they sell friendship and security. Their music and programs are as likely to be market tested as they are to be examined for orthodoxy. There is nothing wrong with finding a community where we fit or which fits us, but such communities and the attachments they engender are easily shed.

Try this thought experiment: Imagine life somewhere in medieval Europe. What might life have been like had you lived there? The chances are you would have been a subsistence farmer, because if there was to be enough food most people had to farm and because this is what your parents did. The family was the basic economic unit. But the village was important as well. Some of the land you farmed might have been held in common and its produce shared.

You would have lived in or near a small village. You would know pretty much everyone you met. You would be unlikely to travel far from your home. The moral authority in your village was the church whose priest was likely to be barely literate. There were local authorities who were likely to be large land owners to whom you owed certain duties and who owed certain duties to you. Central authorities were distant from you and largely irrelevant to your life. As a rule you preferred this.

There were many dangers. The wars fought by the nobility were among them, but probably your main worries were sickness and starvation. Existence was fragile. Life was short. There was little commerce because there was little surplus product to trade and little division of labor. There were some cities and cosmopolitan places, but you were not likely to ever see them. Everyone you saw was pretty much like you.

In this world, communities were "thick." Everyone knew everyone else. The people you worked with were the ones you played with and worshipped with. Life was lived locally. Status was inherited and hierarchical. One knew one's place. Each niche had its duties and privileges. Interactions were infor-mal. They were norm-governed, but not rule-governed. Life was governed by shared understandings about how things were and how things work–by tradition. Attachments to the group were strong. They were rooted in shared understandings, shared identities, and a common fate. Loyalty was to family, kin, place, church. Hostility to those with other understandings and identities could also be strong. People did not see themselves as autonomous individuals. They saw themselves as members of a group. Their world was enchanted–governed by spiritual forces.

This was a world with many dangers but also many emotional securities. In such worlds people might have lived on the edge of poverty and starvation, but they were not lonely. As German sociologist Ferdinand Tönnies (1881/1988) wrote in his classic treatment of this topic, "in Gemeinschaft (community) with one's family, one lives from birth on, bound to it in weal and woe" (pp. 33–34).

In modern developed countries, this world is largely gone. Our communities are "thin." We are members of diverse and partial associations where we associate with different people. We associate in banks, the work place, schools, and places of worship. Few of these associations have an unquestioned power to shape identity or establish firm guidelines for life. We may be different people in different places. Life is not lived locally. We live in a global village, but the global village is not really a village. It is achieved through television and the Internet, but it is not a local community where we interact with the same people in multiple venues against the background of a shared culture. It is a place of vast resources and multiple options, but also of ephemeral relationships, anonymity, and loneliness–a place where it is easy to get lost or to hide.

In our world, status is achieved, not inherited. We may strive for a wide range of occupations and aspire to many diverse roles which we change easily. While race and socioeconomic status are powerful forces inhibiting social mobility, almost no one feels obligated to inherit the station of his or her parents. Our outlook, if not always the reality of the matter, is meritocratic.

Many of our interactions are structured by formal rules and governed by bureaucratic organizations. We comply more than we commit. Shared understandings are not strong; they are easily changed, often contested, and often group specific. We interact with a lot of people with whom we have weak shared understandings–so we have to learn how to respond to "difference," and those who are different are different in multiple and shifting ways. Life is lived with strangers. We move and leave friends, family, and community behind–often. Even spouses are transitional. People see themselves as individuals leading their own self-chosen lives. They may draw on received cultural resources, but they pick and choose as seems good to them. Our communities are the products of free associations. Even those we inherit are easily shed. We live in a moral and aesthetic cafeteria.

This world has been disenchanted. Even deeply religious people do not think that God runs the weather. There is no Baptist chemistry or Jewish math—a good thing, but one that weakens the claim of these communities on us. Religions and philosophies may still provide guidance in life, but there are no longer effective overarching worldviews. Even our cognitive lives are fragmented and partitioned.

Our economic lives are characterized by an extreme division of labor and specialization. In our economic life we deal with one another through arm's-length contracts in which each of us seeks to maximize our own benefit. It is a world where we compete for our standing and welfare with strangers. There is no economic commons.

This is a world that has given us much. We should not look backward with great nostalgia to the emotional security of the small village or small town. But our world can also be one of loneliness, a world of fractured norms and weak relationships, a world in which we are associated with others in many communities but where few have a great hold on us—a world in which, as William Galston (1991) has said, "The greatest danger to children in modern liberal societies is not that they will believe in something too deeply, but that they will believe in nothing very deeply at all"(p. 255). Tönnies calls this world *Gesellschaft* (society). It is a world, he says, into which we go "as we go into a strange country" (p. 34).

What created this world? This is not a story to be told in a few pages. But a few observations will be helpful. Part of the story is technological development, which produced enough wealth to make division of labor and specialization not only possible but required and made formal schooling necessary. The industrial revolution required free and mobile labor. It concentrated labor in cities where neighbors can be anonymous and communities ephemeral. Technological advances in transportation and communication opened a wider world—a world full of difference, strangers, and novelty. We now live in a world that is a marketplace of ideas and alternative life styles; we have much to choose from, but little guidance as to how to choose wisely.

Another force driving these changes is the emergence of capitalism. This not only produced great wealth for many, but it transformed all of us into commodities and market actors. We are individual laborers who have to sell our labor on the market for the going rate. We engage one another through arm's-length contracts in which each views the other as pursuing his or her own self-interest. The ethos of capitalism is YOYO rather than WITT. Isolated individuals lead economic lives dominated by impersonal forces they rarely understand and are unable to control.

Another force is the Protestant Reformation. Protestantism is an individualistic and egalitarian religion where freedom of conscience, a private relationship with God, and the doctrine of *solo scriptura* have undercut the authority of the church. It has spawned innumerable variations. We now shop religions to find one that fits rather than submit to the authority of the "faith of our fathers" or of our church. One of the most important consequences of the Protestant Reformation was the destruction of a privileged relationship between the church and the state. In a place where there is only one "true" faith, that faith can be the moral compass of the state, and the state can promote its interests for the sake of the community. In a place where there are two or more competing religions, the idea that the state should be bound to one of them is a formula for unrelenting strife. The solution is the separation of church and state—one of the greatest achievements of our culture. Religion-based morality becomes a private matter. We must seek another ethic for the state, one that is consistent with what Rawls (1993) calls "durable pluralism." We need a civic ethic we can share with those of other faiths or no faith. If we ascribe to both a civic ethic and a traditional religion, we must become morally bilingual, and we run the danger of becoming morally schizophrenic.

The emergence of liberalism is another factor. Liberalism taught us that we are all free and equal. No one has a natural right to rule, and no one is a natural slave. It helped dissolve the ancient regime where people had a natural place. John Locke (1689/1960) taught that government rests on the consent of the governed and that the legislature is sovereign. Liberalism emphasizes rights against the state. It emphasizes individuality over group membership, and it expects the state to be neutral among different conceptions of the good. Associations are valued, but they must be free. Religion is fine, but it may not be imposed by the state. The state is not a community; it is a means to regulate the competition among free individuals.

Here, too, these developments have given us much. I would not willingly live in a world without jet planes and the Internet, without freedom of religion, speech, and association, and in which authority was inherited. I am a citizen, not a subject. Yet there is also loss. I would prefer a democracy energized more by WITT and less by YOYO. I would prefer one where religious communities and other associations are free, but also deeply meaningful and able to provide real moral insight and guidance. And I would prefer a world in which I had many loyal friends and a loving family (which I have), and where my children did not (as they do) live in different states and countries. These things, however, are conveyed through strong communities. We lack such communities.

All of these factors impact schools. The school is a separate place from home, work, or church. Secondary schools are often separate from neighborhoods as well. Schools need to accommodate diverse populations, people of different religions, races, and ethnicities. Schools are full of strangers. If there is to be community, often it must be constructed de novo.

Schools must decide what to teach and how to teach in a culture where there is little agreement about what kind of learning is worthwhile. They must try to tell children the truth in a society that is skeptical about truth and that can be deeply anti-intellectual. They must try to affirm what is best against the influence of a popular culture that can worship musicians who can barely manage three guitar chords and athletes and actors who are morally challenged. And schools must serve the capitalist state by generating the human capital that supplies its corporations. At the same time, they must create democratic citizens and resist the plutocracy that always threatens states that wish to be both capitalist and democratic.

Schools must serve diverse populations while respecting liberal neutrality. They must make decisions under the direction of a complex educational bureaucracy that is bound by numerous legislative mandates and the decisions of a variety of courts. So our schools emphasize compliance rather than moral authority. They try to serve everyone without resolving the cultural differences that create different interests and different values. They talk about a market place of ideas, but flee controversy and fear debate. American schools tend to privatize the goals of education, to be everything to everyone, and offer a curriculum that is given an instrumental justification. They are like an educational cafeteria; they lack coherence. Our schools have a tacit ethic of possessive individualism: get learning to get more education to get good jobs to get stuff. Their central norm is equality of educational opportunity, a norm that is rooted in the assumption that schools are sites of competition for social goods. Schools accept this role and seek to make this competition fair.

These schools serve some students well and many poorly. They best serve children from homes where the value of education in the marketplace is understood and the skills of negotiating complex institutions have been mastered. They do not succeed on their central norm, equality of educational opportunity. The education they provide produces grossly unequal results. It does not educate good citizens. Nor does it provide students much guidance as to what life is for or how to find meaning in it. These schools are often highly bureaucratic places lacking moral authority where few students have close relationships with a caring adult and where the ethos is dominated by various peer cultures. It is hard to see that the modern secondary school is a community, an emotionally safe place, or a place that can easily transmit a sense of what is right or good.

Thus the dilemma: Community is necessary to good education, but our society has greatly weakened community and makes creating community in schools difficult. I want to know how to create strong and good educational communities in a world that has multiplied communities but has made them thin and weak. And I want to know how schools can be communities in such a world without sacrificing the good things this world has given us. And I want to know how schools can effectively transmit democratic norms and a sense of the kind of lives worth living in institutions in which the capacity to endorse what is praiseworthy is weak.

COMMUNITY AND THE
COMMUNITARIAN CRITIQUE OF LIBERALISM

One reaction to the loss of community in modernity has been the emergence of an ethic called *communitarianism*. Communitarians claim that the goods that constitute human flourishing and the excellences and virtues that enable the realization of these goods reside in the purposes, norms, traditions, and attachments of communities. Hence to weaken community is to weaken the potential of societies to transmit their heritage. The fundamental task of even the most progressive education is thus to conserve what is best and most valuable from the generations that have preceded it. So far I agree. But there is more.

Communitarians see a threat to the viability of communities and hence to cultural transmission in the liberal political philosophy that we have inherited from the Enlightenment. Liberalism deludes itself, communitarians argue, in holding that there are universal moral norms that can be discovered through the power of reason and that can substitute for the norms received from our communities. Communitarians claim that such universal norms that are not the norms of any particular community are a myth. There is, they claim, no "view from nowhere" (Nagel, 1986), no set of universal principles that hold for all times and places. There are only norms that are social creations maintained by human communities.

Communitarians have also accused liberals of postulating a featureless self, one characterized by freedom and reason and constructing itself through its own rational and autonomous choices (Sandel, 1982). This self too, they claim, is a myth. People are socially constructed by internalizing norms that live only in the traditions and purposes of our communities. If we postulate that there are universal moral norms discoverable by reason and if we think that people are autonomous and self constructing, the consequence is that we do not care for the communities where norms and goods live, and we dissolve the traditions and bonds that hold communities together, leaving anomie and alienation in their place. Without community, communitarians argue, people are robbed of their roots and their traditions and become victims of the market—rational egoists and possessive individualists.

The representation of liberalism in the communitarian critique is suspect. There are few recent defenders of liberalism who believe that unencumbered and isolated selves are either possible or desirable or who fail to recognize the importance of norms received from our communities (see Walzer, 2005). Indeed, I doubt that the communitarian characterization of liberalism adequately describes the views of the founders of modern liberalism such as John Locke or John Stuart Mill. Locke's (1689/1960) picture of a social contract arising from a state of nature, a picture that had profound influence on the Declaration of

Independence and the American Constitution, is not an account of the origins of society. It is a thought experiment that forms part of the justification of the authority of democratic government. The point of the state of nature is to deny that there is any natural authority, to deny that we are natural slaves. It is not to deny that we are social beings. When one reads Locke's writings on education (Locke, 1693/1964) or religious tolerance (Locke, 1689/1946) it is clear that Locke saw people as shaped by culture, tradition, and community.

Modern liberals have not been engaged in a project to discover a "view from nowhere" that is binding on all rational agents. They have been trying to discover a view of justice capable of being shared by people in a society characterized by durable pluralism. Most liberals want to hold that in a society characterized by durable pluralism, norms of justice must be norms for everyone. They can only reflect the distinct outlook of a particular subcommunity at the price of domination and oppression.

People are undeniably shaped by their communities and motivated by their attachments. No liberalism that finds these facts false or problematic and seeks their remediation with a healthy dose of autonomy and the "view from nowhere" is likely to be adequate. The trick, therefore, is not to defend the "view from nowhere." It is to develop a form of liberalism in which community, tradition, and attachments count, but in which justice is the justice of all. This project is one that communitarians should share.

Once it is granted that liberals believe that people are shaped by culture, tradition, and community, it follows that liberals have an interest in the quality of the communities available to people and in the effectiveness of institutions that transmit praiseworthy norms. These cultures and traditions are the resources from which good lives are created. If they are not worthy and just, or if their norms are not effectively transmitted to the next generation, people will live lives that are demeaned and unjust. Thus liberals should care about good and strong communities. They should also advocate for cultural forms and practices that create good liberal citizens, and they should worry (as they do) about cultures, communities, and traditions that are illiberal or base.

If there is a communitarian critique of liberalism worth pursuing, it is this: Developing a sense of justice and a worthy conception of a good life depend on the internalization or appropriation of cultural and intellectual resources that live in our various cultures, traditions, and communities. These cultures, traditions, and communities may be more or less worthy, more or less accessible, and more or less authoritative. Liberalism, however, may create institutions and practices that make the richness of various cultures, traditions, and communities more accessible, but less authoritative. If so, the moral authority and, ultimately, the coherence and cohesiveness of robust communities may be eroded by liberal practices and institutions. We need to find ways to value autonomy, free association, criticism and debate, and diversity while also having our children shaped by communities that are coherent and that have the moral authority to succeed in the task of normation–a difficult task.

How might liberalism do this? Many liberals argue that the state should be neutral among competing conceptions of a good life. This means, liberals claim, that the state cannot be a community, nor can it advance the interests of one community over others. John Rawls (1999), the quintessential liberal, supports this view:

> I believe that a democratic society is not and cannot be a community, where by community I mean a body of persons united in affirming the same compre-hensive, or partially comprehensive doctrine. The fact of reasonable pluralism which characterizes a society with free institutions makes this impossible. This is the fact of profound and irreconcilable differences in citizens' reasonable com-prehensive doctrines, religious and philosophical conceptions of the world, and in their view of the religious and philosophical conceptions of the moral and aesthetic values to be sought in human life. (p. 3)

This view has considerable merit, but it does not preclude a society with rich communities other than the state, and it is easily misapplied to the edu-cation of children. We do this, for example, when we think that any attempt to raise children in the norms of a particular culture or a particular religious tradition is a form of indoctrination. Even Robert Ackerman (1980), who is quite insistent that the state must be neutral among competing conceptions of the good, also claims that children need some measure of cultural coherence before they are asked to engage the full diversity of a free society. We also mis-apply liberal ideals when we view schools as marketplaces of ideas but do not see them as places where children should be firmly grounded in traditions of scholarship and democracy which have substantive values of their own.

If we understand notions such as intellectual liberty and autonomy as rights students have against schools, we may turn schools into places where all values can be expressed but none affirmed. Schools that do this throw their students into a cafeteria or shopping mall of cultural goods with no guidance as to how to choose among them. Schools that are unable to affirm some positive values are likely to fail at the task of normation and are likely to be overwhelmed by the popular culture. They may well create students who are rootless, egoistical, and anomic. We need to find ways to create schools that are both intellectually open and able to defend what is true, just, and good–a difficult balance to achieve.

A coherent liberalism, therefore, must seek to create a society that is free, but also one where healthy communities that support shared norms of justice and have a praiseworthy conception of human flourishing are effective in transmit-ting their norms to the next generation. Modern liberals–perhaps because of their commitment to neutrality, intellectual openness, and free association–have been overly suspicious of strong communities. They are not altogether wrong about this, but they have not attended adequately to the importance of strong communities and to the conditions under which such communities can thrive.

THE "BADS" OF COMMUNITY

Liberals worry that strong communities are likely to have certain undesirable consequences, consequences that I will call the "bads" of community. Not every community is a good community. There are certain goods that communities tend to promote. These include trust, loyalty, and a sense of belonging. Communities can provide moral coherence and a kind of emotional safety. But communities may also promote certain "bads." Whereas healthy communities transmit worthwhile norms, some communities transmit norms that are debased or unjust, for example, the Ku Klux Klan. Thus one way in which a community can be a bad community is that the values that unite its members are bad values.

There are other "bads" that are a danger in strong communities. Communities can be parochial. Communities can indoctrinate. Communities can oppress their members or dominate them. They may be total communities inhabited by true believers. Communities can transmit suspicion or hatred of nonmembers. They can be intolerant.

There is a dilemma here. A community is an effective endorser of norms when it is what I have called a "thick" community. Thick communities have two central features. First, they have rich social relations. People interact in multiple dimensions. Social relations between adults and children are caring and age vertical. Children are influenced more by adults than peers. Second, thick communities have norms that are life orienting. They convey a powerful conception of what is right and wrong, good and bad, worthwhile or debasing.

The dilemma is that as communities become thicker, they run a greater risk of producing the "bads" of community. We want a society characterized by communities that are strong and effective, but we want people to be able to move freely among them and learn from more than one. Community must be combined with mobility and intellectual openness. We want communities that are good at encouraging trust and loyalty and the emotional security of membership, but we do not want communities that create intolerance or suspicion of others.

So when we try to create good educational communities, we need to find ways to create strong communities that are effective endorsers of worthwhile norms without creating the "bads" of community. How are we to do this?

Suppose we consider a few metaphors. A community might be like a family, a guild, a congregation, an orchestra, or a tribe. To characterize a community as like a family is to say that it is held together by affective bonds; it is, as some schools claim to be, a community of caring. But this has limits as a picture of school communities. Members of school communities are generally not related to one another. They may be comparative strangers. They may come from different backgrounds. It is not necessarily an easy thing to create strong bonds of caring among strangers. This is particularly true if the relations among students are competitive or if students come to the school from significantly different cultures. A second concern is that the fact that people care for one another does not establish a coherent sense of educational purpose. People who care may still sharply disagree about what they want to accomplish. I would conclude that the family-like school has a picture of a community that is too thin. It relies on a capacity to create caring apart from shared purposes. The fact that it has no shared conception of a good education apart from caring suggests that its capacity to engage in effective normation may be weak.

At the other end of the continuum is the tribe. Tribes (in my metaphorical use of the notion) are characterized by two features. First, members interact with one another in different and diverse venues. They tend to live, work, worship, and play together. Second, they have a shared culture or a shared religious or philosophical outlook. Hence the Amish are tribelike, some small towns are tribelike, some Native Americans (but not all) may live in tribes, and a religious boarding school may be tribelike. Tribes are by definition thick communities. They are likely to do the task of normation well. Indeed, they may be too thick and may run a great risk of the "bads" of community such as parochialism. They can threaten the autonomy of their members. I believe that there are conditions under which we should support schools that are tribe-like–when, for example, the cultural survival of a group is threatened–but I do not think we should aspire to have school communities that are tribelike for most students. Generally such communities are too thick.

This leaves us with communities that are guildlike, congregation-like, or orchestra-like. Guildlike communities are rooted in a shared practice such as mathematics or poetry or carpentry. A school that was a guildlike community would have a curriculum that was focused on a practice or a grouping of practices: Examples are a school of music and the fine arts or a school of math and science. A school that was like a congregation would have a strong shared core-value system. The Friends school I described in the preface is an example. A school that was like an orchestra would have a project focused on a special area of interest or concern, where members tend to succeed or fail as a group, and where cooperation was thus paramount.

Are schools that are like guilds, congregations, or orchestras too thick or too thin? Schools that are communities should have elements that are suggested by each of these metaphors. They should focus on practices, they should share some core values (but not all), and they should emphasize cooperation.

These things help make them thick and enable the work of normation. Are they too thick? They can be. If the practice they emphasize is made too central they can be parochial, or if the values they share are all encompassing or taught in the wrong way, they can lead to indoctrination and intolerance.

At the same time, there are reasons to suppose that they are not too thick. Their social relations are thick, but not too thick. In urban areas a school of music and the arts or one that emphasizes ecological sustainability or one that focuses on creating a democratic community may still begin as a group of strangers. And such schools can be fully inclusive except insofar as the values of core practices are concerned. A school of the fine arts may not wish to admit philistines, but it may admit people regardless of race, class, or religion. And if all schools that are communities are tempered by a strong sense of being an intellectual community and being a democratic community, the "bads" of community will be largely overcome. These kinds of metaphors suggest ways to create communities that can do the work of normation, but are not so thick as to produce the "bads" of community.

SCHOOLS THAT ARE COMMUNITIES
AND SCHOOLS THAT ARE NOT

The modern high school offers abundant access to cultural and intellectual resources, but at the same time its capacity to endorse what is worthwhile is weak. The modern high school has been characterized by some (Powell, Farrar, & Cohen, 1985) as a cafeteria or a shopping mall in that it lacks focus and coherence. It is a place that values knowledge instrumentally. Adults rarely agree on the value of the education they collectively offer. Roles are formally defined. Authority is hierarchical. Rules are followed (when they are) because they are official rather than because people feel their moral force.

In the modern high school, goals tend to be privatized. Students do not see themselves as junior members of communities of practice motivated by the goals of these communities or as members of democratic communities motivated by a sense of WITT. They see themselves as acquiring knowledge and skills that they will use in pursuing their own individual life goals: getting into a good college, getting a good job. Knowledge and skills are instruments to achieve private and individual aspirations. Thus the school is not a community. It is more like a bank, a service provider, or a cafeteria—a dispenser of goods that passes no collective judgment on their worth.

In the modern high school, community is not formed around the mission of the school. Often there is no mission on which the adults who run the school can agree. Students are lonely and seek community in peer groups. The influence of adults is diminished, while that of Madison Avenue and MTV is enhanced by the age segregation of the modern high school and its lack of connection to the adult world (Coleman, 1974). The modern high school student lives in a world where Budweiser, Bach, football, faith, love and lust all compete for attention, but it is a world with few guidelines for choosing wisely and a world where the ability of adults to effectively endorse norms is weak. Moreover, the least praiseworthy of the goods and goals that bombard our youth are likely to be backed with the most resources and the most sophisticated techniques of persuasion.

The modern high school is often neither nurturing nor coherent. It is often a mass bureaucratic institution characterized by multiple and conflicting purposes. Students in the modern high school feel themselves to be strangers and are often alienated and anomic. They see adult expectations as an alien force arrayed against them. Compliance must be obtained by incentives and punishments. Passive resistance is common. There is little sense of intergenerational shared purpose.

Bryk (1993), appealing to the work of sociologists Philip Cusick and Christopher Wheeler, provides this characterization of the modern "reformed" high schools. It is worth quoting at length:

> "Reformed" high schools convey a distinct vision of a society in which individuals strive for personal success while pursuing their self-interest. Institutional norms are competitive, individualistic, and materialistic. Although the private vision of teachers may be broader and more humane, it is the institutional norms that are continuously reinforced by daily school life.
>
> Much of this enculturation is conveyed through the differentiated curriculum, student tracking, and teacher assignments. Not only do such academic structures produce an inequitable social distribution of achievement, but they also socialize students to internalize the cause. . . .
>
> Enculturation in public schools also occurs through routine social encounters. Such encounters are regulated by explicit codes of conduct that specify prohibited behaviors and elaborate individual rights to be ensured. These codes define the minimum standards of social order necessary for the academic work of the school to proceed. Few see them as an embodiment of the ideal of justice or any other ideal. (pp. 318–319)

These schools are creatures of the society in which they exist. They express the norms of liberal capitalism where the aims of life are largely private and people are seen as engaged in competition for the resources required to realize their own self-chosen conception of the good life. They see people as members of the species *homo economicus*. Education is seen as largely a matter of getting a good job with a high income that enables one to purchase desired items in the market. Knowledge is a commodity to be acquired and sold in the labor market. Its value is in part determined by how much of this commodity is possessed by others.

This outlook on life and on education produces schools that are not communities. They have these essential characteristics:

1. Goals and aims are largely private. The main goal of the school is to provide a curriculum that serves diverse private aims without significantly altering or critiquing them.
2. Because the curriculum aims to serve diverse and private goals, it is incoherent. There is no shared educational project.
3. There is a significant division of labor. Teachers are departmentalized and see themselves as subject matter experts; they view their primary responsibility as the transmission of their area of expertise. They lack a broader commitment to the school's overall educational program.
4. Social relations among students are competitive, and knowledge is seen largely as a commodity.
5. Tracking contributes to the failure of many students. At the same time, it legitimizes failure and the justice of its consequences by creating a veneer of meritocracy.
6. Behavioral norms emphasize compliance and individual rights rather than a shared conception of justice and common goods. Students tend to see behavioral norms as imposed and civil rights as protection against the demands of the school (Strike, 1978).
7. Trust and care may occasionally exist between individual teachers and students, but they do not flow from any sense of shared purpose. Students and teachers alike are inclined to see the behavior of others as self-interested rather than oriented toward achieving shared purposes. Hence incentives are important in securing compliance.

Such schools are not inevitably "bad" schools. They may in fact be quite successful in such tasks as graduating a high percentage of their students and getting them into good colleges. They are especially likely to be successful if their students come to school having internalized the norms of competition and success through academic achievement from their families and communities. That is, such schools may serve the interests of academically talented middle-class students well. They serve the interests of other students much less well. But successful or not, they are not communities. They are more like banks or shopping malls—places that exist to serve private aims, whatever they are.

Schools that are communities have different characteristics:

1. They have shared goals expressed in a publicly acknowledged shared educational project.
2. The curriculum they provide has coherence because it expresses shared goals.
3. While there is some division of labor involved in different subject matter expertise, teachers are not highly departmentalized. They teach their subjects so as to express shared goals, and they see their task broadly as one of achieving the school's overarching mission rather than as one of communicating their subject matter.
4. Students come to understand and internalize the shared project of the school and see themselves as cooperating with teachers and one another in pursuit of shared aims. Knowledge is valued for its contribution to the understanding and appreciation of experience and its contribution to justice and citizenship. It is not merely a commodity.
5. Tracking and electives are minimized in favor of a shared curriculum and other shared experiences intended to create community.
6. Behavioral norms flow from shared goals and a shared conception of justice. The school has moral authority because teachers and staff are seen as acting from commitment to shared aspirations.
7. Trust and care are seen not only as features of the relationship between some individuals, but as flowing from shared commitments.

These contrasting pictures are ideal types. In fact, we live in a liberal capitalist society where goods and services are distributed through markets. In an advanced technological society knowledge is a commodity; and further education, jobs, and income should largely be allocated meritocraticly. A school that failed to prepare students to succeed in such a society would not be a good school, no matter how much of a community it was. Any school must be a bridge to its student's success in this society. Hence creating a school that is a community is a matter of striking a delicate and complex balance.

In this chapter I have presented insights into the major problem to be solved. Community is necessary because authentic teaching and effective normation depend on strong communities. Communities need to be thick enough to succeed at the task of normation. At the same time communities can be too thick. They can create the "bads" of community. So the core question is, "How do we create schools that are thick enough to do the work of normation, but not so thick that they produce the "bads" of community?"

In Part II of this volume I argue that right now the small schools movement has the best answer to this question—at least potentially. But first I need to develop the idea of schools as communities more fully, especially in terms of normation and a shared educational practice. Then I present a more detailed look at two particular forms of community: communities of practice and democratic communities.

CHAPTER 3

Schools as Communities

A community is not formed every time a group of people happen to interact with one another; true communities are bound together by the values, norms, and experiences their members share. The deeper and more strongly held those common values, the stronger the sense of community.
—Francis Fukuyama, *The Great Disruption*

Good school communities should be thick enough to endorse praiseworthy norms, but not so thick as to create the "bads" of community. In this chapter I want to expand on the idea of normation and to develop the idea of what I call a "shared educational project" as crucial to schools that are neither too thin nor too thick. This shared educational project helps create the four Cs of community: coherence, cohesion, care, and connection.

COMMUNITY AND NORMATION

Several decades ago, when open education and free schools were trendy reforms, I attended a meeting of free school enthusiasts. A featured speaker was an articulate young woman of age 15 or 16 who told how she had been oppressed by her former high school. She claimed that her school had had a lot of pointless rules and made her study a lot of "irrelevant" stuff. Now, however, she attended a free school. She had few rules or expectations to cope with, and she studied topics of her own choosing. Since she studied only what she was interested in learning, she was learning a lot. The audience seemed to find her pronouncements persuasive.

The people who attended this meeting shared a common vision of a good education as well as a common culture. Like the students in the Friends school I mentioned in the preface, they spoke a common language. Their language was full of allusions to repression and freedom. It had its heroes and its enemies. Paul Goodman, Jonathon Kozol, A. S. Neill, Carl Rogers, and Paulo Friere were discussed with reverence. "Regular schools" were referred to with contempt, as prisons staffed by fascists. There was even a uniform of sorts, if long hair, jeans, and tie-dyed T-shirts can be considered a uniform. I felt this shared culture strongly since, wearing a coat and tie and not applauding at the proper times, I was obviously a nonmember. Mistrustful glances were exchanged.

These individuals formed a community of a sort. And they had succeeded in socializing the students who attended the free schools they operated into its culture quite effectively. The students they had in tow were all in uniform and were able to speak the language of the movement with considerable competence and enthusiasm. The irony of their conformity about freedom escaped them.

In the question period that followed the young woman's brief talk, it did not occur to anyone to ask her what she was learning, whether what she was learning was of genuine worth, or whether she had learned what she was learning very well. Yet there were reasons to treat her claim that she was learning a lot with considerable suspicion. She had noted in describing the freedom she had achieved that her liberation included the absence of any expectation that students would arrive at school at any particular time. It seemed that they drifted in during the morning and that the morning was often devoted to socializing or singing folk music. There were classes in the afternoon. Attendance was optional. Students did a great deal of independent work (she claimed) on topics of their own choice. Whatever the merits of these educational practices, they did not seem characterized by much time on task or by efforts at systematic instruction. The idea that anyone was accountable to anyone for anything would have been anathema.

Nevertheless, the people in the room took her claim to be learning a lot as self-authenticating. Perhaps this was because they believed that ultimately the individual is the only judge of the value of what is learned. "I'm free to study what I want, so now I'm learning a lot" might border on being a tautology.

This young lady was highly alienated from her previous high school. One imagines that her disaffection was abetted by her initiation into the student culture of the late 1960s. In my mind she has become a kind of poster child for the claim that "alienation is the problem." Curiously she is also a poster child for the claim that "community is the cure." I do not mean that she was learning a great deal about math, science, history, or English. I doubt that she was. At the same time, she was not alienated from the culture of her new school. She had internalized its norms. She could speak the language with conviction, and she strongly identified with the adults in her school and their values. If her education was not effective in the conventional sense, it surely was effective in socializing her to this alternative culture. Whether or not her new school had taught her much, it had plainly cured her alienation—at least from her current school.

The free school movement typified one line of thinking, individualistic in rhetoric and communitarian in practice, about how to deal with alienation.

Such schools often saw themselves in the Romantic tradition of Rousseau (1762/1911), which emphasizes learning that is self-motivated and, because it is rooted in the self, is authentic, not alienated. When students are self-motivated, they will own their education because it is a form of self-expression, and they will be engaged with learning because they are learning what they want to learn.

In recent years another response to student disengagement is more likely to be given: What students need is high expectations set for them by adults. These high expectations are expressed in the form of standards and are often enforced through high-stakes tests. We are sometimes told that one reason why American students appear not to do as well as students in other countries is that little turns on how well they do (Bishop, 1989; Shanker, 1994). High-stakes tests on which something such as employment or further education turns thus provide incentives for achievement.

In this case what children should learn is determined by three considerations. The first is an assessment of what is known. We want what we teach to be current, up-to-date, the best available, world-class. The second consideration is an assessment of children's long-term interests (not what they are currently interested in, but what is good for them). We want our children to learn what they will need to know and be able to do in order to be successful adults. What they need to be successful adults is strongly associated with their successful pursuit of higher education and entry into the job market. The third consideration is the public good. We need to teach our children what they need to know to be productive citizens. Here too the central purpose of the school is assumed to be the formation of human capital, but now the emphasis has shifted to the public interest in productivity and competitiveness.

Given such criteria, there is little reason to believe that children's untutored preferences for what they want to know would regularly lead them to study what they should learn. Indeed, while these criteria do include the long-term interests of children, none of them makes reference to what children currently want to learn. Educators may hold that it is pedagogically important to make some connection with students' current interests, but the point is to get past current interests so that students are learning what adults think is good for them and for society. Since students' interests do not lead them to study what adults believe they need to know, they need incentives of some sort. Incentives, it seems, are the modern reform movement's answer to student disengagement. They are also, it seems, a substitute for self-motivated learning.

There are responses from the Romantic tradition to such arguments. It may be claimed that excessive use of incentives virtually guarantees that students will be alienated from learning, even if they seem compliant with adult expectations. Indeed, students may experience incentives as a form of coercion. In schools dominated by standards and high-stakes tests, there will be little done from the love of learning.

Moreover, Romantic critics may claim, focusing on a student's immediate interests will not lead to a curriculum that ignores the long-term welfare of society or of the child. Bridges can be built that connect the child's current interests to what adults have decided is worth learning, and society is not benefited by creating large numbers of alienated people. Students who learn by following their own interests will ultimately learn to be good judges of what their interests are. They will be better and more productive citizens because of this.

This is an old and unproductive argument. Both sides have their points. But both sides ignore the extent to which wants and needs are social products and that membership in communities is the primary way in which the socialization of wants and needs happens. We all really know this. We see the connection between community and what people want, value, and believe expressed in human activities from cooking to religion. People tend to like the food of their culture, worship the god of their parents, and play the games of their neighbors and friends. They speak the language of their community and internalize its patterns of thought. Language shapes not only how we think and see the world but also what we want and hope for (Dewey, 1916). Who we are, and who are ours, are questions central not only to what we feel we need and want but to how we think about the meaning of our lives. If so, perhaps the crucial educational question is not whether we should permit students to follow their interests or generate incentives for them to do what adults believe is good for them; instead, the real question is "How can we help students see the education they are offered as expressing a praiseworthy set of goals and values that they share with us because they are the goals and values of praiseworthy communities of which we and they are members?"

If we ask this question, we will not simply let students study what they want. Nor will we see ourselves as getting children to learn what we have decided is good for them. Instead, we will see ourselves as sharing with them practices that are of value. This question warrants setting expectations for children by adults, but it also seeks to avoid disengagement and alienated learning by seeking to develop a community of shared educational commitments with students. As Aristotle (ed. 1941) noted long ago, education must shape the character of people so that they love what is admirable and hate what is shameful. How do we do this? We view educating as a process of initiating students into a variety of communities.

Consider an illustration. An article entitled "Young Math Competitors Honor a Hero" in the July 15, 2001, issue of the *New York Times* describes a meeting of mathematically talented youth:

Dr. Andrew Wiles, who has rarely appeared in public since solving one of the most famous mathematical problems of the ages, was greeted like a rock star by the current generation of young math stars at the close of their global competition.

Dr. Wiles, famous for his proof of Fermat's Last Theorem, was met with whoops and sustained applause Friday by hundreds of young people who took part this week in the International Mathematical Olympiad, the most prestigious high school mathematics competition in the world. (p. 12)

These students are atypical in that they had shown a remarkable talent for mathematics. At the same time, their identification with someone whom they saw as a member of their community who has had significant success in achieving goals that their community values is not unusual. We see this kind of identification all the time in sports and music. People sometimes respond in similar ways to revered religious figures. The question to be asked is how this happens. How do students internalize the norms that inform the subjects we teach in school so that they care about them, identify with their goals, and feel a bond with their competent practitioners?

These math students have internalized what Alisdaire MacIntyre (1981) calls the "goods internal to practices" in that they understand and care about the aims and aspirations of math. Hence, they can admire someone who has furthered these aims and aspirations. They are exceptional in their talent, but I do not believe that one must be a math prodigy to care about math and to express hero worship for a math star any more than one has to be a basketball star to care about a well-executed pick and roll or want to "be like Mike."

Here is a classroom example. Ms. S. was my high school algebra teacher. She was a good teacher, not so much because she loved teenagers, although she did seem to like them, but because she loved math. One of her joys was to share this love with others. I recall a day when she put a proof on the board. She "proved" that $1 = 0$. "Clearly, this cannot be right," she said. "Then what's wrong with the proof?" We discussed this for most of the class. We checked the proof carefully. We could find no mistake. After a while, we had to know. She provided a few hints. Finally, we discovered that in one line of the proof we had inadvertently divided by zero. "Well, why not divide by zero?" we wondered, and we were off on another inquiry.

What was Ms. S. doing? Many things no doubt. But three are crucial. First, she was engaged in authentic teaching. She was not just teaching facts and computational skills; she was showing students what doing mathematics is like and doing so in a way that engaged their natural curiosity. Second, she was teaching in a way that affirmed the worth of her students through her evident desire to share something of value to her with them. Third, by engaging in authentic teaching, she helped initiate students into the community of mathematicians. She had put their feet on the path to membership.

Note also what she was not doing. She was not trying to motivate students to learn mathematics by attaching some mathematical concepts to their current interests. I doubt any student in her classroom would have had any interest in why one should not divide by zero at the outset of the exercise. Nor was she motivating through incentives. There was no test, no reward for solving the problem, and no punishment for not doing so. While she may have been relying on natural curiosity, she was creating interest where there was none by showing what there was to be interested in about mathematics and by affirming us in our emerging interest.

We should learn four things about normation from this example:

1. Normation is crucial to both excellence in learning and engagement with learning.
2. Normation changes people. It alters perception, taste, and character.
3. Normation involves initiation into the shared projects of a community.
4. Normation depends on belonging, and belonging depends on normation.

These ideas need a lot of development. Let's start with the question "What is a norm?" Simply put, a norm is a kind of rule or standard. The fundamental characteristic of rules and standards is that they enable us to know when we are doing something right or when we are doing it wrong. If I say "Fido are a good dog," I have violated a grammatical rule. Competent English speakers feel the mistake even if they can't articulate the standard. Rules may be tacitly understood. We need not be able to state them in order to follow them. In fact, often we discover the content of our norms by analyzing our intuitive sense of what is right and what is mistaken, and what is good or bad. Norms and standards pervade our lives and shape our feelings about what we and others do. They enable us to experience beauty and outrage, sympathy and disgust, excellence and ineptitude.

Learning a subject such as math (or science or history or carpentry or football) is not just a matter of learning mathematical facts or even mathematical reasoning. A genuine engagement with mathematics is a matter of internalizing an appreciation for those goods that are integral to mathematics, and genuine competence in mathematics is a matter of developing a commitment to and grasp of those norms important to the practice of mathematics. One becomes a mathematician, in some measure, by learning to care about the elegance of a proof, learning to be engaged by puzzle solving, and learning to worry about and understand what is meant by rigor and consistency. Coming to care about the goods and internalize the standards of excellence of the mathematical craft illustrates what I mean by normation. Green (1999) refers to normation of this sort as the voice of craft.

Normation involves both commitment and competence. It is part of what it means to value a practice for its own sake and achieve excellence in its practice. Ms. S. used the discussion of her proof to show us what mattered about mathematics and to facilitate our normation. Our progress in normation was best shown by the fact that we came to care about solving the problem and about the norms of consistency and rigor in proof. We would not have said it this way, but we did come to care about these things.

Mathematicians are able to see the world in new ways. They care about things that others do not care about. Their character is changed. Concern for rigor and elegance, argument and evidence–the ideals of the craft–become part of who they are.

Normation alters perception, aspirations, taste, and character. To come to value the goods internal to a subject matter and care about its norms is not a private matter, just as learning a language is not a private matter (Wittgenstein, 1953/1986). It is to come to share a common project with others and be initiated into the community of those who share its goods and norms. It is to affiliate.

Mathematicians are not just people who are skilled in mathematics. Collectively they are members of a certain form of community, a guild of sorts, and, as such, the "owners" and custodians of its goods and standards. Their shared practice of their craft, their debates, and their scholarship are where these goods and standards live and develop, where they are refined or challenged. Their activities keep these goods and norms alive and nurture them. To learn mathematics is to begin an apprenticeship to the accomplished members of the mathematics community and thereby to begin an affiliation. Ms. S. was not just a good math teacher. She was a good recruiter. Good teachers are missionaries and emissaries for their communities.

A sense of belonging both aids and is aided by normation. That we are included, that we belong, is a significant factor in our willingness to internalize the norms of a community. That we internalize these norms also becomes a factor in our inclusion. Community begins in learning the norms of those who care for and about us, and ends in caring for and about those whose norms we share.

Ms. S. illustrates these points. Her teaching typically began with an invitation to her students for them to be included in the practice of mathematics. Indeed, to enter her classroom was to enter the temple of mathematics. She regularly invited us to share in its mysteries by engaging us in the solution of problems to which the norms and goods of mathematics were important and through which they could be displayed. Her lessons showed what is central to mathematics. They exhibited such goods and norms as the value of an elegant proof, the fascination of an apparent paradox, and the importance of insisting on consistency and rigor. She did not argue for these things. She did not even name them. She just showed us what counted with mathematicians. We were not just invited to study math so that we could get a good job or get into a good college. Such justifications, whatever their merit, miss the goods internal to math. They also tend to conceptualize colearners as competitors for scarce goods. They exclude rather than include. Instead, Ms. S. invited her class into a community through the shared pursuit of common aims, the solution of puzzles, which, if they could not be solved, would pose a challenge to the norms of consistency that are central to mathematics.

Finally, Ms. S. showed us that we were valued by sharing something that was important to her. Her evident desire to share something she loved enabled us to trust her. Her message was, "Here is something that human beings have found to lend value to their lives. Try to see it as I do and perhaps you will be enriched as others have been. And I will be enriched if I can share this with you." The trust and the sense of affirmation inspired by an evident desire to share what one has found worthwhile is a crucial element in initiating students into intellectual communities. Trust is inspired when teachers are able to create a sense of community where all are part of some larger "we" pursuing a shared aim.

Ms. S. was engaged in authentic teaching. If we teach mathematics as merely a collection of facts, theories, and skills, and we do not show its norms and goods, we misrepresent it. In effect, we lie to students about what we are teaching. To teach subjects properly–authentically–requires that we show their norms to students. To learn them authentically, students must not only grasp their facts, theories, and skills, they must come to understand and value what they are for.

Authentic teaching is teaching that faithfully represents what is taught by showing it to be a human activity with internal goods and norms of excellence, the mastery of which allows us to achieve these goods. Authentic teaching may or may not require real-world contexts. Its primary aspiration is to represent the subject matter faithfully, not to connect subject matter to students' current interests. It is to transform them. It would be odd, for example, to try to teach civil engineering apart from real-world contexts. That would not be faithful to its point. But much of mathematics has little real-world application. Ms. S.'s teaching was not authentic because it used real-world examples–there were none in the example I have provided. It was authentic because it engaged students with the kinds of activities that mathematicians engage in and showed the norms that inform their activities. Teaching mathematics–or anything else–authentically is teaching it in a way that is not reductive. Authentic teaching shows practices to be human activities with their own norms, goods, and excellences. Teaching them authentically shows this. That is what Ms. S. was doing.

COMMUNITY AND SHARED EDUCATIONAL PROJECTS

If students are not to be alienated, schools must be places that communicate a sense of belonging by inviting students to participate in a shared educational project. What is a shared educational project, and how do we invite students to share in it?

A *shared educational project* has four elements. First, it is a vision about what might be called "the greater educational goods" that can be realized through a good education. Do not translate this into the cliché that communities are formed by shared values. They are, but educational communities are formed through shared values of a particular sort. Most people in schools value good plumbing, but unless they are enrolled in a school for plumbers, that is unlikely to create an educational community. People in schools may value individual success, but that is more likely to dissolve community than create it.

Nor does an aspiration for higher achievement or a conviction that everyone can learn–important as these may be–add up to an adequate vision for a school that wishes to be a community (Strike, 1999). Such aspirations and beliefs do not tell us what academic achievement is for or why we believe it to be important that all children learn. If such aspirations and beliefs are linked only to goals such as getting good grades or getting into the right college, they can dissolve community by emphasizing scarce positional goods for which students must compete. Having an adequate vision of the nature of a good education involves, in some measure, having a shared picture of a good society and a shared vision of what is best in life. We need a vision of the role of education in human flourishing.

The second feature of a shared educational project is that the shared vision must be expressed in shared activities through which people cooperate in realizing aims that are rooted in the shared vision. Ms. S. believed that our lives would be enriched were we to internalize the goods and norms of mathematics. That was her vision. The puzzles and problems she set before us engaged us in shared and cooperative projects that helped us realize this vision. In her class we engaged in the shared practice of mathematics. We did not engage in the individual acquisition of the scarce resource of mathematical skill.

The third feature of schools that have a shared educational project is that such schools have a shared language that all members of the community–not just the staff–use to justify and describe their shared practices. In the preface I mentioned a visit I once made to a Friends school. One of the things that characterized this school was the fact that certain aspects of a Quaker outlook provided a common vocabulary employed by all members of the community to discuss their shared project. Students were able to think of what they were doing as "seeking the spark of God within." As I noted earlier, I do not think many of the students and staff took this phrase literally. For most, it merely meant that they should look for and seek to cultivate the best in others. What was important was that this shared language provided a framework for deliberating about their common life in the school. Moreover, the school had collective practices, including regular all-school meetings, through which this language was acquired by the students. It is important that this language was substantive enough to produce some coherence in the deliberations of the school but was also flexible and vague enough to allow the school to include those of diverse backgrounds.

The young lady mentioned at the beginning of this chapter who spoke at the meeting of free school advocates had also acquired the shared vocabulary of a shared project. She knew how to talk about being oppressed and freed up and how to describe the practices of her new school in this language, just as the students in the Friends school could discuss their school's practices in the language of Quakers. I have seen similar shared languages in democratic schools, schools emphasizing a particular subject area, Afrocentric schools, Catholic schools, and schools for at-risk students.

That a community has a shared vision and a common language does not ban contention. In any institution in which there are human beings there will be disagreement. What makes communities different is that the shared vision and the common language provide a framework for deliberation about disagreements. Having a shared vision means that there is a better chance that deliberations can produce reasoned consensus, thus diminishing the role of power and procedure in decision making.

The fourth element of a shared educational point is this: Community is established when many of the shared activities that flow from a shared vision of a good education are of a sort such that people can—perhaps even must—succeed together. Shared educational projects are cooperative learning writ large. Ms. S.'s puzzles were of this nature. We worked on the problem together. When we solved it, we all knew the answer. On the way, we taught one another.

Some useful examples of groups whose members succeed or fail as collectivities are athletic teams and musical organizations. When schools are communities, they are like orchestras. They can only play well by playing together. Of course, members of orchestras may compete for chairs and solos, and members may play different instruments and different parts. Community bans neither competition nor difference. At the same time, members of communities pursue goals that they can only achieve as a collectivity, and each member benefits from the success of all. Hence each should care about the success of all. In community, trombonists care about oboe players.

These four features of a shared educational project make a strong case that schools that are strong educational communities should have a curriculum that expresses a shared set of educational values and that all students take. Community is created by shared activities that assume shared norms. This means that there should be a core curriculum (specific to a given school) that all students take so that they have a common experience in their school (Bryk, Lee, & Holland, 1993), that tracking should be minimal, and that electives should not be so numerous as to undermine a common experience. When a school wishes to be a community the entire school must be engaged in a process of authentic teaching in which the norms that underlie the community's shared education program are shown and its shared language is taught.

Different schools may have different shared educational projects. We live in a society characterized by durable pluralism. Moreover, different curricular emphases will enable us to create schools that have a better fit to the aspirations of diverse families and the needs of diverse children. If we are to have schools that have a coherent sense of their mission expressed in their distinctive shared educational project, we must also have different schools with different projects and offer choice among them.

At the same time, there are certain foundational goals that all schools should aspire to. They should, for example, aim at individual autonomy: the capacity of students to make thoughtful and wise judgments about their lives independently. And they should aim to produce good citizens with a concern for social justice and the common good. These goals require an education that is both humanistic and democratic. And they require that schools be communities that are intellectual communities where ideas are valued and democratic communities where all members are valued equally. Every school, regardless of its shared educational project and the distinctiveness of its program, should aim at these goals and should strive to be an intellectual community and a democratic community. While we may want schools that are diverse and that have different curricular emphases, we also need to have a unity of core purpose in this diversity.

There is a conception of human flourishing involved in goals such as autonomy and citizenship. It sees a part of the human good as consisting of intelligent self-direction and another part as involving life in democratic community. Nussbaum, (1990) has described such a conception as "thick, but vague." It has substance, but it can be expressed in various ways. It is consistent with diverse cultures and religions—not all to be sure. When a culture or religion is anti-intellectual or antidemocratic, schools must stand their ground and defend a reasonable conception of a good education. It is the commitments to the worth of intellectual practices and democratic community that are key to having educational communities that are thick enough to do the work of normation, but not so thick so as to produce the "bads" of community.

If we cannot share goals rooted in the goods internal to the practices we teach and in democratic values, then, in order to have a curriculum at all, we will need to emphasize the instrumental characteristics of knowledge. Thus, in effect, we will say to our children, "You are free to conceive your lives as you choose. You may understand human flourishing as it is understood in your religion or your culture. In this school we say nothing about what life is for. We do not agree among ourselves about this. We merely provide you with knowledge that is likely to be of value to you whatever life you choose. It does not matter who or what you want to be, you are probably going to need to know how to read, some mathematics, a bit of science. Moreover, the welfare of society depends on your knowing enough of these things to be a productive citizen. But what you value in life, what you think these bits of knowledge and skill are for, is up to you."

While we are unlikely to actually say this to our students or to ourselves, nevertheless we often act as though this was the truth of the matter and thereby effectively communicate this message. We do this by departmentalizing and compartmentalizing the education we provide, by tracking, by offering numerous electives, and by emphasizing the economic value of what we teach.

Like banks and shopping malls, many schools are places in which people come together and engage in forms of cooperation in pursuit of ends that remain private ends. In a bank, one person may be saving for a vacation or for a child's education and another person borrowing for a car, a house, or a boat. We do not need to agree on the ends we pursue so long as we agree that saving or borrowing are means to their pursuit, and we do not need a common language to discuss our purposes. Hence banks may be functional organizations, but they are not communities. The ends of those who use them remain private, not shared. They share no common language. After Babel (Stout, 1988), what remains is commerce and a trade language.

We need not accept this kind of response. Within the scope of the goals that all should share, we may diversify educational communities so as to allow individuals to pursue interests about which people legitimately differ. The trick is to encourage diverse schools with different shared educational projects and to permit choice among them. This permits particular schools to be more focused and to emphasize their own distinctive vision of good education. Schools may emphasize the arts, or science and math, or a particular vocation, or ecology or social justice. They may have an international or a multicultural emphasis. In contrast, schools that seek to satisfy everyone's interests will be fragmented and incoherent.

The creation of more focused schools may require us to abandon the aspiration to have comprehensive schools, but it does not require us to abandon the common school outlook in which we seek to create good citizens by providing a shared education to diverse students. The common school outlook does not require that every student study the same thing everywhere. It requires that students who come from different backgrounds study together.

Public schools that are communities can provide programs and curricula that provide substantive quality education for all in groups that are religiously, racially, and socioeconomically diverse. If these schools have a distinctive focus, they will not and should not be inclusive in one special sense. They will have distinctive educational values, and they will select students who do or can share these distinct values. But they can and should be inclusive in all other ways. A school of ecology, a school of the arts, and a school of equine science can each enroll people of all races, religions, and ethnicities.

THE FOUR Cs OF COMMUNITY

Schools that are communities have what I shall call the "four Cs" of community: these are *coherence, cohesion, care,* and *connection.* Having a shared educational project helps create these four Cs. Coherence consists in having a shared vision, a shared language and shared activities rooted in them: a shared educational project. Cohesion is the sense of community that results from the common pursuit of such a project. Care is required for initiating students into this project. Connection provides the structure for the community. Much of the preceding discussion has been about coherence and cohestion, but we need to discuss care and connection more fully.

Care

There is danger that the idea of care will be reduced to a kind of warm and fuzzy notion best expressed through hugs and smiles. Not that there is anything wrong with hugs and smiles. But we need a more robust view of what it means to care for students. Part of this notion is to express our care as Ms. S. did, by sharing something of value with students. This means that we must care about their authentic learning, about enriching their lives through learning. It is noteworthy that some scholars (Shouse, 1996) have found that a caring environment without a strong emphasis on academic success actually harms the achievement of some students, especially poor minority students. We do not benefit our students with a form of care that resists making demands on students because we fear to harm their self-concept.

Care includes moral expectations. Raywid and Osiyama (2000) comment in a paper discussing the shootings at Columbine in 1999:

> We need to deliberately cultivate in schools the qualities associated with *accep-tance*, such as empathy and compassion. . . . these traits must be both modeled by staff members and deliberately cultivated among students. The major ways of cultivating them are, first, through the personal relationships that constitute school communities, but also through what is taught–certainly in the humanities. Literature can instruct eloquently in kinship, empathy, and compassion,

as can people's history, to cite just two examples. Over the years, schools have tended to focus on making youngsters more informed, more rigorously trained, more skilled. Perhaps we had better begin focusing on also making them more humane.

Finally, the relationship between care and community needs to be emphasized. There is a "dialectical" relationship between care and community (Strike, 2008). Care helps to establish the kind of relationship between adults and students that helps initiate students into community. Care is essential to the creation of communities that are able to effectively endorse worthwhile norms. Community once established helps make the bonds of care deeper. The fact that people share common goals and values and that their identities are shaped so that they begin to see themselves in others creates conditions under which friendships can flourish and strong bonds can be formed. Care and community are thus mutually reinforcing.

This dialectical relationship between care and community, in its ideal form, can be expressed in a series of when/then situations:

When individuals are cared for, then they come to feel a bond with their caregivers. They want to emulate them and be respected by them. And they come to trust them.

When these caregivers are also in a mentoring relationship with young people and when they represent a particular community or culture, then these young people will be motivated to become a member of that community or culture, to master its practices, and understand and internalize its norms and goods. They will become initiates.

When these initiates progress in the mastery of the practices and the internalization of the norms and goods that characterize the community or culture represented by their caregivers, then their membership in this community or culture is increasingly a function of shared experience, shared capacities, and shared norms and goods. They begin to see themselves in others and others in themselves. They begin to share a common identity.

When new members are well initiated into the community or culture, then they begin to take on roles appropriate to full members and their standing in the community is maintained by a shared understanding of how members think and behave, by the belief that they share common purposes with other members, and by trust that others will fulfill their roles. Community thus comes to be maintained by reciprocity with respect to common purpose.

Finally, when new members feel themselves to be full members of the community, then they come to care about other members in other, deeper, and non-instrumental ways. And they become able to care for and mentor new initiates.

Thus the process of reconstituting community across generations begins and ends in caring, but passes through the sharing of understanding and purpose. This process is the primary (if not the only) way in which people come to love the gods of their community and enjoy the food of their culture. It is also how people become musicians, carpenters, and physicists. It is how schools build community around a shared educational project.

Connection

The fourth C of community is connection. So far, I have emphasized what might be called the conceptual and affective requirements of community, but community also has "structural" requirements. People need to be in regular contact with one another in ways that build understanding and trust.

There are five requirements of connection. The first is scale. Schools should be small enough for their members to get to know one another. It is particularly important that students get to know some adults well. It is, however, important to be clear that, while smallness is a precondition of community, good educational communities do not occur simply because they are small. Instead smallness increases the chances that community can be created. Good educational communities first and foremost are created by shared purpose. Schools can be small and still surround kids with adults who lack any common purpose. And they can also be little bureaucratic fiefdoms.

Second, schools that are communities need to have "flat," nonbureaucratic, democratic, and local organizational structures. Scale is very likely a precondition of this. Most organizational theorists (Lee & Smith, 1997) claim that bureaucracy increases with organizational size. Schools need to be small enough to be run informally rather than bureaucratically. Trust and moral authority need to be emphasized over compliance.

The third requirement is that schools that are communities require social structures that are more age vertical than age horizontal (Coleman, 1974). Students need to be well-known to caring adults. These relations need to be more important in their school experience than their connections with their peers. Normation works best when the norms of a community are communicated to the next generation by those who care for them.

The fourth requirement is what has been called "intergenerational closure" (Coleman & Hoffer, 1987). Parents and other adult members of the community need to be able to get to know one another so that adults reinforce the shared values of the school, not only for their own children, but also for others. Schools that are communities need to be a bit more like small towns or church parishes. Intergenerational connection is not just a matter of the relations between teachers and students. It concerns the relations between parents and other significant members of the community as well.

The final requirement of connection is stability. Community will be difficult to create with a constantly shifting cast of characters. Small schools in urban areas are not like rural schools in one very important respect: They are usually not the extension of a larger community outside of the school. They are not creatures of the town, the parish, or the neighborhood. This will be especially true when they are themed and when there is a public choice system.

Such schools face the problem of quickly creating a sense of community among people who are often strangers and may be characterized by significant racial, ethnic, socioeconomic, and religious diversity. Creating community will not be easy if we have a constantly shifting cast of characters. Schools that are communities thus need to give thought to how they can hold their students and keep their staff.

What is crucial about these four Cs is that community is more than warm and personal relationships between students and teachers, and it is more than having a flat and democratic organization. We can have these things and not change what goes on in the classroom or how students learn. First and foremost, what makes a school a community is that its "citizens" share a common educational agenda that is carried out throughout the school–in its classrooms as well as in the manner in which it conducts its affairs. It must also be carried out in a school where all are valued equally.

Schools that are good educational communities are intellectual communities and democratic communities whatever else they are. They must value inquiry, dialogue, and evidence. They must be just and inclusive. These are demanding conditions. The anonymity and mobility of our society militates against them. But this makes them all the more important.

CHAPTER 4

Community of Practice and Intellectual Community

The unexamined life is not worth living.
–Socrates

Let us hope . . . that by the best cultivation of the physical world beneath and around us, and the best intellectual and moral world within us, we shall secure an intellectual, social, and political prosperity and happiness, whose course shall be onward and upward, and which, while the earth endures, shall not pass away.
–Abraham Lincoln, Address to the Wisconsin State Agricultural Society

The way children best learn the complex skills and dispositions of adulthood is through keeping real company with the kinds of experts they hope to become (and, incidentally, through keeping company with the real things of the world–the malleable and predictable–although occasionally surprising–stuff of which the world is made). Amazingly we no longer trust these ways of learning.
–Deborah Meier, *In Schools We Trust*

In this chapter I explore the ideas of authentic teaching and learning in more detail, and I will discuss the goals of education that are associated with them. What we want, I argue, are schools that view themselves as communities of practice and intellectual communities. We want schools that initiate students into practices that enrich their lives.

Authentic instruction emphasizes learning from others in a way that is like an apprenticeship. It is often, as Meier suggests, learning by keeping company with experts, and learning by engaging the real things of the world.

Schools that are communities of practice and that emphasize authentic teaching have a humanistic educational project: that is, they are committed to a vision of education that aims at goals that go beyond the conventional economic goals that currently dominate educational policy debates. We should want schools to create good citizens who are able to manage their own lives and make reasonable choices about how they will live in a society that provides a bewildering array of choices but little guidance about how to make them wisely. And we should want schools that do more than enable children to secure the material conditions of life. We should want schools that give children the capacity to enjoy experience–to see and value what is worthwhile and enriching. And we should want schools that help children to live well with others–to establish rooted friendships and enriching communities. These are the kinds of things–along with the democratic aspirations that I will discuss in Chapter 5–that constitute a humanistic education. The goal is to do more than train productive workers. It is to create people who are able to lead flourishing lives.

What kind of education enables children to grow up to be adults who are able to flourish? In one respect my answer to this question is quite conventional. The kind of education we need wants students to be meaningfully acquainted with music and art, literature and languages, math and science, and history and the social and behavioral sciences. It also values sport and craft. However, we need not provide this education in a conventional way. We should prefer depth to breadth. We should encourage schools that are themed in some way and that use their theme to integrate various subjects. When a student develops a passion for some particular part of the curriculum, we should encourage and indulge that passion. Schools may emphasize ecology, equine science, aerospace, or biotechnology and still teach history and literature well. Indeed, they may teach them with more success if they are able to weave their school's theme into these subjects.

One of the ironies of modern school reform is that we have placed enormous emphasis on teaching academic subjects. At the same time we have taken these components of what was once called a liberal education and taught them in illiberal ways. We have emphasized their economic purposes over their humanistic purposes, and we have distorted the notions of rigor, excellence, and standards in such a way as to delude ourselves that passing tests that emphasize information recall constitutes a good education. We use the elements of a humanistic education to dehumanize.

COMMUNITY AND THE CORE GOALS OF EDUCATION

Consider some ideas generated by one of the groups that has been most supportive of the small schools movement, the Coalition of Essential Schools (2006). This organization has 10 Common Principles that guide the work of associated schools:

1. Learning to use one's mind well
2. Less is more: depth over coverage

3. Goals apply to all students
4. Personalization
5. Student-as-worker, teacher-as-coach
6. Demonstration of mastery
7. A tone of decency and trust
8. Commitment to the entire school
9. Resources dedicated to teaching and learning
10. Democracy and equity

These principles express in a succinct way much of what I have and will argue for. The first two, for example, capture a great deal of what I mean by authentic teaching and learning. But we need to think them through.

Why should we wish to use our minds well? The development of our minds enriches our lives not only because it enables us to get jobs and income, but in other ways. As Abraham Lincoln suggests, a good education is one that cultivates the best intellectual and moral world within us. Lincoln made this remark in a speech intended to promote the use of scientific agriculture—a most practical venture—but he had a broader vision as well. So should we. Why should we want to use our minds well? What does it mean?

One of the foremost nineteenth-century philosophers, John Stuart Mill (1863/1961) answered these questions this way.

> There is no known Epicurean theory of life that does not assign to the pleasures of the intellect, of the feelings and imagination, and of the moral sentiments, a higher value as pleasures than those of mere sensation. . . .
>
> [Hence] it is better to be a human being dissatisfied than a pig satisfied; better to be Socrates dissatisfied than a fool satisfied. And if the fool, or the pig, is of a different opinion, it is only because they only know their own side of the question. (pp. 408, 410)

There is, to be sure, more than a whiff of elitism in Mill's comments, but we should consider what lies behind them. Mill is developing a view of human flourishing—of a good life. An Epicurean theory is one that claims that the good life consists in pleasure. Mill is making the case for the kinds of pleasures that require developing our minds and our skills.

We need to understand this in a way that is not elitist and that does not translate into the idea that the best life is one of contemplation rather than of activity. Such a view is an ethic for a leisure class, one in which others do the work. Instead we need to understand Mill's ideas as concerning the kinds of activities that are experienced as valuable simply in the doing of them and as a view that tells us what we should look for in our work as well as in our leisure.

Given this, why might we find that the pleasures of the intellect, and of the feelings and imagination, and of the moral sentiments, lead to a life of flourishing? What makes them better than a life dominated by "mere sensation"?

Consider the words of Socrates (quoted in Plato's *Apology*). "The unexamined life is not worth living." This is overstated. We all know people who seem to enjoy their lives and who rarely examine them. For some, ignorance is bliss. But perhaps Socrates had something else in mind: Plato's dialogues (in which Socrates, who never wrote anything, is the lead character) suggest that the examined life is important if we are to be liberated from two kinds of cognitive slavery or servility. The first is slavery to our own desires. If we are to be able to live good lives, we need to be able to rule our desires instead of being ruled by them. This means that we need to be able to examine what we want and to ask whether what we want is genuinely good for us. Moreover, we need to develop the capacities that will allow us to act on our decisions once we have made them. Reflectively lived lives are better lives because we act to secure what is genuinely good for us.

Second, we need to be able to escape the servility that can be imposed by the blind acceptance of received tradition. While we may end up accepting the traditions we receive from our parents or our community, we need to make these traditions ours. We do so by reflecting on them and choosing them (or rejecting them and choosing others) for our own reasons. If we cannot do this, we are slaves to our culture or our religion. I call the capacity to examine our desires and our traditions and to change them for reasons *autonomy*. Autonomy is something that most people find admirable and desirable about themselves as well as a precondition of choosing wisely and well in a complex world. Autonomy requires that we use our minds well.

Good citizenship also requires that we use our minds well. Citizenship is not just voting. It is engaging our fellow citizens in a reasoned and collaborative search for justice and the common good. Good citizenship requires us to use our minds well.

The full enjoyment of experience also requires that we use our minds well. This is, perhaps, the core of Mill's claim above. Philosopher John Rawls (1971) puts it this way: "Other things being equal, people enjoy the exercise of their realized capacities (their innate or trained abilities), and this enjoyment increases the more the capacity is realized, or the greater its complexity" (p. 426).

Rawls is suggesting that people tend to enjoy doing what they have become good at and that when they have a choice between two activities, they generally enjoy the one that calls more on their capacities and requires more complicated and subtle judgments. He illustrates this by comparing chess and checkers. Someone who is able to play both with reasonable skill will generally prefer to play chess because it is the more complex game and evokes a higher level of capacity than does checkers. We might say something similar about music. People are more likely to enjoy listening to or performing music when doing so requires discernment and skill–provided, of course, that they have acquired the capacity for such discernment and skill. And we should say that same thing about work. Jobs that are varied and that elicit and develop our capacities are more enjoyable than those that are repetitive and involve only easily mastered skills. Enjoyment of experience requires us to use our minds well.

The quality of our relationships also requires that we use our minds well. We live in a morally complex world. Ethical and fulfilling relationships require more than mere goodwill. They require the ability to be perceptive about others–what they are thinking and feeling and what they need–and it requires the ability to think through morally ambiguous situations.

Moreover, relationships are often formed around common interests and within communities of common interest. People who like chess are likely to find friends in chess clubs. People who like to perform music may find their friends in orchestras or choirs. To put this point in a different way, our friendships often grow from the relationships formed within communities of practice. These relationships depend on our mastery of practices. They require us to use our minds well.

These things are not a full account of human flourishing. A good life depends on health and love, for example. But they do suggest things that can be addressed by education. Thus they suggest some goals that should be core goals of an education that focuses on all of the things that enable a life of flourishing, such as the following:

1. Every school should promote individual autonomy.
2. Every school should create good citizens.
3. Every school should develop the capacity to enjoy experience.
4. Every school should develop the capacity to interact with others in ways that are ethical and that contribute to the quality of relationships.
5. Every school should develop the capacity of individuals to earn a living and to enhance the productive capacity of society.

These goals are best advanced by a curriculum that gives pride of place to academic subjects authentically taught and that includes a significant component of the arts and humanities as well as mathematics and science. Of course some of these goals are also advanced by mastery of things that are not academic subjects. Goal 3, for example, may be advanced by sports and crafts, and schools should not neglect these. However, it is the arts, humanities, and sciences that develop our minds in the ways required by such goals as autonomy, citizenship, and the ability to think through complex ethical issues. And while sports and craft can enhance our capacity to enjoy experience, so can music, literature, and the arts. A good education emphasizes these subject areas.

We also need to develop the productive capacity of students. A society that does not transmit its productive skills to the next generation dies. However, life is more than production. We must all do productive work, but a life that is dedicated to nothing more than work is likely to be narrow and unfulfilling. So is a life that is reduced to production and consumption. The life of a possessive individualist is stunted. Good lives are created by the capacity to enjoy what human beings have found to be of greater worth—art, music, and literature, as well as craft and sport. The appreciation of these things is learned. Sophistication is required.

Moreover, a focus on intellectual activities that are experienced as worthwhile simply in the doing, that help create autonomous people and good citizens, and that help develop friendships and ethical relations, is community developing in a way that an emphasis on the economic goals of education is not. Unlike goals such as getting into a good college or getting a good job, goods such as autonomy, citizenship, or an enhanced capacity to appreciate experience do not require us to compete for them. They are not scarce goods. They may be rare if they are difficult to achieve, but this does not make them scarce. There is not a pool of autonomy where if I get some there is less for you. My capacity to appreciate Mozart does not diminish yours.

Indeed, the opposite is the case. Such goals are best pursued in community because in good educational communities the achievement of each individual furthers the achievement of all. Autonomy is moved forward by discussions among intelligent and perceptive people. In music, we are likely to appreciate more and perform better if we are members of a community devoted to producing good music. When we have a shared educational project, the other person is our benefactor, not our competitor.

Finally, economic productivity may be enhanced by an education that does not overly emphasize it. Some philosophers have noted that happiness is not best attained by the direct pursuit of happiness. People who pursue their own happiness frequently find themselves in an escalating spiral of increasing want and unfulfilled desire. Ultimately their wants cannot be satisfied. They always need more and better. They make themselves into people who are selfish and unfulfilled. In contrast, those who are most likely to be happy are those who are engaged in some project that they pursue because it is worthwhile.

Economic productivity is like this. Craftspeople are more productive when they are motivated by a sense of satisfaction in a job well done or when they care about the beauty of the object they are producing. Someone I know well is an engineer. He works for a major corporation in operations research. He works in supply chain management, a most practical activity. If I want to annoy him, I tell him that he is a glorified shipping clerk. But he has shown me the spread sheet that he has developed that handles complex data about the supply chain and makes recommendations about such matters as manufacturing schedules, warehousing, and shipping. The equations he has developed are complex and well beyond my grasp. He takes great pride in his work and finds doing it well a source of satisfaction. He enjoys problem solving. He is also a natural teacher because he finds satisfaction in showing others how to use the tool he has developed and takes pride in their mastery. What motivates him in his work is not just his salary or the stock options his company provides, it is pride in a job well done, the opportunity to develop and express complex skills, the enjoyment of the puzzle solving that his work provides, and the opportunity to share it with others. He is a more productive employee because he is motivated by noneconomic goals.

We need an education that understands this. We will have a more productive economy if we do. And we will also have an economy that provides meaningful and rewarding work because we have produced people who care about it.

If we are to succeed in realizing these noncompetitive and noninstrumental goals, it matters greatly how subjects are taught. They must be taught authentically. And they must be taught in a way that is community constituting. This is to say that they must be taught as practices.

THE IDEA OF A PRACTICE AND THE TRANSFORMATIVE CAPACITY OF PRACTICES

I have talked a lot about practices, but what exactly is a practice? Alasdair MacIntyre (1981) characterizes a *practice* as

> any coherent and complex form of socially established cooperative human activity through which goods internal to that form of activity are realized in the course of trying to achieve those standards of excellence which are appropriate to, and partially definitive of, that form of activity, with the result that human powers to achieve excellence, and human conceptions of the ends and goods involved, are systematically extended. (p. 175)

Examples of practices include complex games and sports (e.g., chess and football), academic disciplines (e.g., mathematics and biology), the arts (e.g., musical performance, dancing, and painting), many occupations (e.g., farming and engineering), and most crafts (e.g., pottery and wooden canoe making).

There are six features of practices that I want to discuss in depth. First, practices are community-dependent human activities. They are things people do, and they are things people do together. The pursuit and achievement of the goals of practices requires cooperation. Moreover, the sustainability of practices depends on a community of practitioners that maintains and extends them and initiates new members. We pursue the goals that are internal to practices cooperatively, and we often achieve them together or not at all. Even in activities that seem to involve a great deal of time alone, practices are community-dependent. For example, good poets may spend a lot of time writing in their studies or in private contemplation, but poets write within a received tradition–or in opposition to it. They have learned the skills of poetry, the aesthetic standards of poetry, and the point of poetry from others. Other members of the community of poets have helped them hone their skills through teaching or critique. When poets manage to redefine what poetry is or what it aims at, they do so against the background of current understandings, and they must persuade others to see things differently. Much the same can be said of any practice from physics to farming.

Second, practices aim at the realization of goods that are internal to them. Science, mathematics, and literature aim at understanding, each in its own unique way. Art, music, poetry, and craft aim at beauty as well as understanding. Even the most practical of complex activities have goods that are internal to them. Farming may aim at the production of food, but farmers take pride in a well-tended field or healthy animals. I have relatives who are dairy farmers. They produce milk. But they are involved with their animals in noninstrumental ways: They show them at fairs and take pride in their grooming. They are part of a community that is culturally and aesthetically involved in dairy farming in ways that go well beyond the requirements of production. For them farming is a way of life. Their practice creates a community that benefits them in many ways. It is a source of friendship and social support as well as occupational support.

Third, practices achieve their ends through the development and mastery of excellences. Excellences are skills and capacities. They may involve the mastery of complex ideas, theories, and cognitive skills. They may involve knowing facts as that is conventionally understood, but the relevance of facts is that they enable excellences. The notion that we achieve goods through the mastery of excellences and that these goods are valuable in noninstrumental ways may reasonably be called valuing knowledge for its own sake, but we should be careful how we understand this idea. If we think that facts or theories are valuable merely in the possessing, we are in danger of trying to create people who are more dilettantes than masters of a practice. There is little human value in only being the kind of person who is likely to succeed on a TV quiz show. We want to educate people who are good at and care about human activities that produce beauty and understanding.

Fourth, the mastery of practices extends capacities. People who have mastered a practice are able to do things, understand things, see things, and feel things that others cannot because they have acquired the skills, understandings, and standards of judgment that define excellence in their area of practice.

Fifth, practices involve the internalization of moral and aesthetic norms. Practices are rule-governed activities. They involve such things as understanding rules of judgment and what counts as a valid argument, knowing what is beautiful, and recognizing what counts as doing something well. Thus to be seriously engaged in a practice has moral significance. To be engaged in physics or math or history is to be engaged in the pursuit of truth. Practitioners must respect evidence and argument. They must be willing to change their minds for valid reasons. They must report data faithfully. And they must follow the argument where it leads, not lead the argument where they want it to go. To be serious about a practice is to have internalized these norms–to be committed to them.

Finally, practices are transformative. This is the point that is most important to emphasize here. When someone masters a practice, that person is changed. Not only has one mastered a body of fact, knowledge, and skill, one is able to see the world in new ways. When one has mastered the interpretive skills of literature or poetry, one is able to see the world through the eyes of the author–or even to see it in unique ways that were most likely not intended by the author. When one has mastered the excellences of a practice, one can value the world in new ways. Good mathematicians not only are more likely to get the right answer to mathematical problems, they value rigor in argument. They enjoy puzzle solving. They appreciate an elegant proof. They care about things they were unaware of before. They are transformed.

Practitioners are transformed in ways that go beyond the ability to see, understand, and value in new ways. They have become members of a community whose members are able to see, understand, and value in similar ways. They affiliate. They see themselves in others and others see them as members, people who are literally like-minded. Their identity is transformed. Such affiliation enables other goods, such as friendship: We are able to enjoy the company of others because we share a common bond.

Practitioners may also be transformed morally. Because excellence in a practice requires integrity, those who master a practice may tend to be better people for that reason. They may acquire virtues that are of broad social value.

It is these transformations that are crucial to overcoming alienation and disengagement. When a student has moved along the path to mastery of a practice, what the student wants changes. To see the point of a practice, to come to see the world through the lenses that the practice provides, to care about its goods, and to want to act with integrity is to cease to be alienated from that practice. It is to want to continue on the path to mastery because mastery helps one realize goods that one now values, because one has come to value the kind of person one is becoming, and because the practice is a source of community.

CREATING COMMUNITIES OF PRACTICE

How do we create communities of practice? We emphasize authentic teaching and learning. Authentic teaching is more than effective teaching. It is teaching with integrity. It is faithfully representing the character of the practices being taught. Authentic teaching is not just pedagogically desirable; it is a moral imperative because to fail to teach authentically is to lie to students about one's subject matter.

Authentic teaching and teaching with integrity involve telling and showing the truth about one's subject. This means representing the practice as a practice and representing it in its fullness. If we tell our students that $2 + 2 = 5$, we lie. If we show a picture of mathematics that does not convey that mathematics involves a unique way of pursuing the truth, one that involves valuing rigorous argument, consistency, and appreciating the elegance of a powerful equation, we misrepresent mathematics to them; thus we lie. Authentic teaching requires us to represent the subjects we teach as practices with their internal goods, intellectual and aesthetic standards, and distinct forms of reasoning. Anything less is a misrepresentation. Authentic teaching is a moral requirement, a form of truth telling

Authentic teaching is typically an apprenticeship-like activity or, as the Common Principles of the Coalition of Essential Schools suggest, a kind of coaching. Authentic teaching is not just telling; it is showing. Students need to be shown the standards that apply. They need models of competent performance. They need to see how the goods that infuse the practice motivate the expert who teaches them. They need expert feedback on the competence of their performances.

If we understand the idea of apprenticeship broadly enough, all practices can be seen to require a master-apprentice relationship. Ms. S., my algebra teacher, was showing us what was important in mathematics. She provided feedback on our arguments and analyses. We were her apprentices.

Authentic teaching and learning require the appraisal of real performances. An apprenticeship requires learning through performance and the appraisal of performance by a competent observer. Mathematics is not just calculating; it is problem solving. To learn mathematics is to engage in it under the eye of the expert. It is to learn from the expert's appraisal and critique.

Authentic teaching creates community by initiating students into a community's practice. It creates members who belong. We should think of whole schools, not just classrooms, as built around communities of practice or as integrating various practices around themes. To do so we need to attend to the four Cs of community.

Coherence and cohesion require that we have schools where the staff, students, and parents share a common set of educational commitments. We need to disavow the idea that we need to be all things to everyone. On the contrary, we need to focus. One way to do this is to emphasize a coherent grouping of practices as the school's special concern. A school of the arts and music is likely to attract like-minded students and faculty and to be able to achieve coherence because art and music, while different practices, are linked by a common concern for matters aesthetic. Similarly, we might have schools that emphasize science and mathematics.

Coherence may also be achieved (as I prefer) by looking for themes that help integrate different practices. We might emphasize occupations that focus on some practice or grouping of practices in the way that the health professions, biotechnology, and agriculture are all rooted in biology. Or we might emphasize ecology. Ecology not only involves diverse sciences, but also history and the social sciences: consider the diverse disciplines required to understand recent cap-and-trade proposals. An integrating theme can be used to weave diverse practices into a coherent educational experience. We might do the same in schools that emphasize multiculturalism or social justice. What is required is that teachers work together so that the integrating theme is followed through in various subjects in a planned and coherent way.

Coherence is the mother of cohesion. If the school has a theme of some sort, then it is more likely, for this reason, to produce cohesion because the members of the school community will be working together on a common educational project. There are also other educational practices that should be followed in order to promote cohesion. The curriculum should provide a common experience for all students. There should be no tracking and the electives offered should not be so numerous as to undermine a common experience. Emphasis should be on the similarities among practices or the integration of practices around a unifying theme. Fragmentation along areas of specialization should be resisted, and teachers should not be departmentalized. They need to work together across subjects to enable the coherence of the instructional program. They should view the creation of a coherent and cohesive experience for all of their students as a central part of their obligation.

Care and connectivity must also be emphasized if a coherent curriculum is to be effective in creating the kinds of strong communities that enable normation. Students need to be in long-term relationships with caring adults. These adults must also represent the school's curriculum to their students so that students want to learn because they want to please and emulate their caregivers. Parents and other community members also need to be brought into the school community so as to create intergenerational closure and connectivity with the "real" world.

Good schools provide a special sort of care. They may care for the student in a variety of ways. Teachers may, from time to time, need to be a friend or parent. But the caring that good schools especially require is the kind that Ms. S. showed. She cared for her students by sharing something she valued with them. She was a willing master in a master-apprentice relationship. Caring and connectivity thus hang together with the school's educational program.

Note how well these features of a community of practice fit with the Common Principles of the Coalition of Essential Schools. Authentic instruction involves teaching students to use their minds well. It emphasizes mastery because the goals internal to practices can only be realized through mastery, and it sees a focus on depth over coverage as important to mastery.

Authentic teaching sees the pedagogical relationship as apprenticeship-like. It seeks to show more than tell, and it focuses on performance. Learning is encouraged through feedback and critique. The teacher is, in effect, a coach, and the student is a worker. A student's success is shown by the fact that the student has become an accomplished practitioner of the practice by demonstration of mastery in a performance. The work of teachers is collaborative and not departmentalized. A focus on authentic learning combined with a concern for coherence and cohesion points toward providing a shared experience for students and collaborative work for teachers. There is a commitment to the shared project of the school. Such a commitment encourages trust and cooperation.

Creating a democratic community also helps create communities of practice. Democratic community is a way of expressing the idea that all are valued equally. Democratic community is pervaded by a sense of WITT rather than YOYO. Communities of practice that emphasize the humanistic goals of education over the economic goals of education have a kind of WITT of their own. They are the kinds of communities where people succeed together and where people learn from one another. The success of each contributes to the success of all. People care about each other because they are rooted in a shared project. They are shaped so that they see themselves in the other. They share a common experience in their education. They are more likely to trust because they see others as sharing their goals and as benefiting from their success. Communities of practice encourage WITT. In the next chapter I explore the democratic aspect of strong school communities.

CHAPTER 5

Democratic Community

Creating a Polity

In order to foster a democracy that is reflective and deliberative, rather than simply a marketplace of competing interest groups, a democracy that takes thought for the common good, we must produce citizens who have the Socratic capacity to reason about their beliefs.
–Martha Nussbaum, *Cultivating Humanity*

Segregation of white and colored children in public schools has a detrimental effect upon the colored children. The impact is greater when it has the sanction of the law; a sense of inferiority affects the motivation of a child to learn. Segregation with the sanction of law, therefore, has a tendency to retard the education and mental development of negro children and to deprive them of some of the benefits they would receive in a racially integrated school system. . . . We conclude that in the field of public education the doctrine of "separate but equal" has no place. Separate educational facilities are inherently unequal.
–*Brown v. Board of Education* (1954)

IF WE WANT DEMOCRATIC SCHOOLS, WHAT DO WE WANT?

Everyone I know is in favor of democracy. Almost everyone I know is in favor of democratic schools. But it is far from clear what it means to be in favor of democratic schools. Americans tend to see democracy as resting on the consent of the governed and believe that consent is expressed through free elections. Is democracy simply electing those who govern us? Are democratic schools simply schools that are run by elected legislatures? If so our schools are democratic.

Abraham Lincoln claimed that American democracy was government of the people, by the people, and for the people. Elections do not give full expression to these ideals. "Of" and "by" suggest a higher level of participation than simply voting. Without significant citizen participation a government "for" the people is paternalistic. A benevolent monarchy might be "for" the people. Lincoln's phrase seems to evoke a picture of a democratic community–one formed by free, self-governing individuals who see themselves as bound together by their collective pursuit of common goods. This requires more than voting.

Nussbaum's comment above suggests that the form that citizen participation takes is deliberation. The aim of deliberation is to achieve common goods. The quote from *Brown v. Board of Education* adds an additional element. In a democracy we value people equally and treat them equally. Perhaps, then, democratic schools involve significant citizen participation, deliberation about the common good, and practices that affirm the equal worth and equal dignity of all. Is this what we want schools to be when we want them to be democratic? If it is, perhaps our schools are not all that democratic.

Public schools are run by a combination of school boards, city governments, state governments, and Congress–elected bodies all. They govern by making policy and hiring employees to implement it. They create public bureaucracies to carry out their will. These bureaucracies are often remote from the concerns of the local school, and they draw effective power from it. But many people who want schools to be democratic think that centralized and bureaucratic control of schools is just what they don't want. They want school governance that is distributed, participatory, and local. Often they see the education bureaucracy as the enemy of genuine democratic governance.

Robust democracies pursue common goods. Citizens see themselves as sharing a common fate and a common future. They make decisions collectively about matters that affect them all. They may seek to expand the range of common goods because this strengthens the community. Robust democracies create goods that improve the community and cement ties among citizens. Parks are an example.

Finally, robust democratic societies value equal opportunity, but they go beyond equal opportunity to ensure that all are fully included and cared for, especially with respect to things that are foundational to human dignity and flourishing. Health care is an example. A democratic society is judged not only by its provision of equal opportunity, but also by the fact that it enables its weakest members to live decent lives with dignity. It sees the provisions it makes for its weakest members as part of the common good. Our schools, however, struggle to achieve equality of educational opportunity, and we are less than firmly committed to democratic inclusion.

So if we want to create democratic school communities, what is it we actually want? I suggest the following definition of *democratic community*:

> A democratic community is a community of citizens who understand
> themselves to share a common fate and see themselves as engaged
> in a common project toward the realization of common goods. It is a

community whose members have shared deliberative procedures for addressing their common problems. It is a community where all are equally valued.

I call a democratic community with these characteristics a *polity*. If we want democratic schools, then we should strive to create schools that are democratic polities. Schools that are polities will give expression to democratic localism. We do not want decision making about our schools to be overly dominated by bureaucracies created by distant legislatures. We want participatory decision making by the members of the local school community. We want the legislatures that govern our schools to forebear and to allow citizens of the local school polity to have a significant role in their own governance.

We also want schools that go beyond equal opportunity. Equality of educational opportunity aims at fair competition. Schools are obligated to provide equality of opportunity. But when competition in the market is the sole determinant of the allocation of economic rewards, some will get little or nothing because they are unable to compete successfully. A genuinely democratic society is one that provides all of its members what they need in order to lead lives of dignity because it values all independently of their productivity in a market society. Similarly, a school that is a democratic school includes all because it values all. No student should be viewed as a second-class citizen of the school. No student has a second-class identity. All students are valued independently of their academic talent and physical capabilities. Not being good at algebra does not make a student less valuable, nor does having a disability.

THE GOVERNANCE OF DEMOCRATIC SCHOOL COMMUNITIES

How should schools that are polities be governed? There are many actors who are potentially involved in school governance. A coherent view must balance the claims of school boards, administrators, teachers, and the families that comprise the school community. I want to argue for a view of governance that locates significant authority in the local school community, the polity.

What role should teachers have? A few years ago there was a strong push to declare that teaching was a profession (Darling-Hammond, 1985) and that professional teachers should have a dominant role in governing their practice. The story went like this: The distinguishing feature of a profession is that it is a community of self-governing experts with significant autonomy and authority over its area of expertise. This authority is justified when competent decision making depends on expert judgment and expert judgment depends on the possession of an esoteric body of knowledge.

The self-governance of professionals may have several expressions. Individual professionals may be self-governing with respect to their own individual practice as doctors and lawyers often are. Professions may also be self-governing in the sense that they are collectively self-regulating. They determine the standards that the profession should uphold and the requirements for admission to and exclusion from the profession. Most important for my purposes here, professionals may work together in a self-governing collectivity that I call a *collegium.*

Teachers form a collegium when they deliberate together about the education they will provide in their schools and when their deliberations are authoritative for their practice. When there is a collegium, teachers teach one another and learn from one another. Practice is improved through deliberation. The relationships among members of the collegium are democratic. Decisions are made though deliberation. Consensus is sought. This is the form professionalism might take in schools.

I believe that teachers should function as a collegium, but I also believe that this version of professionalism does not adequately characterize the role that the collegium should play in school governance.

I am doubtful that the practice of teaching is firmly rooted in any esoteric body of knowledge about education (Strike, 1990; 1993). These doubts are not about the wisdom or skill of teachers, but rather about the state of systematic educational knowledge. There is great disagreement about almost every claim made by educational researchers. Moreover, it seems clear that there are many fine teachers who manage to practice competently without possessing the research-based knowledge that various people have proposed as the basis of a profession of teaching. Good teaching results from subject matter knowledge, experience, consultation, and wisdom more than from possession of a body of esoteric pedagogical knowledge. The most important role of a collegium is to share the wisdom of practice so that it is collectively held.

Since professionalism roots authority in expertise, it is undemocratic. It undermines the authoritative voice of other members of the polity. Professionalism may lead to seeing students and parents as clients rather than as citizens of the school. Clients may have voice, but their voice may be viewed merely as a source of information needed for the decision making of the professional or consent to what the professional has decided is best. But in a democratic polity all members of the community–including parents and students–are citizens, not clients. Their voices should be authoritative in some way.

My final concern with professionalism is that it can be construed to limit the role of teacher to what the teacher is expert about. Teachers may come to see themselves as responsible for teaching their classes, but for little else. What is wanted in a school that is a community, however, is teachers who see themselves as sharing responsibility for the entire school's program and for all of its students. This point is put well by the Coalition of Essential Schools (2006). Here is the full text of Common Principle 8:

> The principal and teachers should perceive themselves as generalists first (teachers and scholars in general education) and specialists second (experts in but one particular discipline). Staff should expect multiple obligations (teacher-counselor-manager) and a sense of commitment to the entire school.

While I do not believe that teaching is a profession in the sense that has been advanced, I do believe that teachers, along with the leadership of a strong and democratically inclined principal, should have the dominant role in creating the educational program of the school. There are two reasons: First, teachers are responsible for teaching their subjects with integrity. Democratic schools should not be able to undermine authentic teaching (Strike, 2005). Second, teachers are the ones who do the work of educating. This fact must be recognized in any adequate view of school governance.

Teachers in public schools are representatives of intellectual communities to students. One danger of democratic localism is that it can lead to parochialism. This is particularly of concern when local values conflict with a faithful representation of an academic discipline.

The cure is to insist that teachers have a special responsibility for maintaining an emphasis on an education that develops the critical capacities of students. Amy Gutmann (1987) in her work *Democratic Education* puts it this way:

> What role should we attribute to teachers? We might conceive of their role as supporting a complementary division of labor between popular authority and expertise: democratic governments perpetuating a common culture, teachers cultivating the capacity for critical reflection on that culture. (p. 77)

Authentic instruction in academic subject matters is the principal mechanism whereby schools cultivate critical capacities. Academic practices are the repository of critical tools and ideas. They are the means whereby we are able to bring thought to bear on our individual and collective lives. Teaching them authentically requires us to employ them as critical tools. When we do so, we develop the mind and create critical capacity.

Teachers must be empowered culturally and legally to teach authentically even if this brings them into conflict with the local culture. For example, one of the hot-button issues of the day is the teaching of scientific creationism or intelligent design as an alternative to evolution. Legally, attempts to mandate creationism or intelligent design have been rejected because federal courts have found that such mandates violate the Establishment Clause of the First Amendment (see *Edwards v. Aguillard,* 1987 and *Kitzmiller v. Dover,* 2005).

There is a different and better reason to reject creationism in schools (Strike, 2005). Creationism does not reflect the views of modern biology and is not viewed as scientifically plausible by the overwhelming majority of biologists. To teach it as a viable alternative to evolution is to lie to one's students about the practice of biology.

If teachers are to teach authentically, if they are to develop the critical capacities of their students, if they are to help students to be autonomous individuals and good citizens, they need to have the authority to teach authentically, and this authority cannot be subject to veto by local democratic institutions. Thus while I believe that schools should be governed largely as local democracies, I believe that the collegium, because it represents academic communities, must be the arbiter of the authentic representation of the practices these communities sustain.

The second reason why teachers have a special role in the governance of the school is that they do the work of teaching, and this work requires the making of judgments that are complex and significantly dependent on context. If decisions about the practice of teaching are made by distant bureaucracies, those judgments are likely to be insensitive to context and will result in an alienated work environment. This is also likely to be the case if the school polity regularly interferes with or overrules the collegium about the school's educational program.

We must therefore seek to redeem the idea of a collegium from the conventional vision of professionalism in a way that renders it consistent with the desire to create a democratic school community and which also respects the obligation of teachers to teach authentically. There are three essential steps in this redemption: (1) to respect the autonomy of the collegium with regard to teaching authentically; (2) to see the relationship between the collegium, where most deliberations about the school's educational program take place, and the parents and students of the school as fiduciary; and (3) to create an authoritative voice for parents and students.

A fiduciary relationship requires loyalty on the part of the collegium to students, their families, the school, and the school's shared educational project. Teachers are expected to place the welfare of those whom they serve above their own and fulfill all of their duties to them. Those who are served by the collegium should, in turn, respond to loyalty with trust. Where loyalty and trust are the basis of the relationship between the collegium and the students and families who are served, details of governance become less important.

A school that is a democratic polity must also have structures and practices that encourage the deliberative participation of students and parents in the governance of the school and that give some authoritative voice to them. They are to participate, not merely to be informed or consulted. This authoritative voice may vary according to role. But even the voices of children should be heard and should count in some way. A school that denies an authoritative voice to its citizens is not a democratic community.

Here are three models of participatory governance:

1. *Town meeting:* Some schools have all school meetings where all citizens of the school meet to discuss issues before the school community. Votes may be taken, but the main point is to discuss issues that are before the school and to seek a consensus about them. Generally, any votes taken are advisory. Democratic schools do not require—and should not have—institutions in which students can outvote their teachers.

2. *School council:* A school council is a representative body whose members are chosen (often by elections) from different groups— teachers, students, parents, and members of the local community (Bryk, 1998). Their perspective, however, should be one in which they seek the best for the school rather than representing the interests of their constituents.

3. *Trusteeship:* In a trusteeship individuals are appointed to oversee the school. Trustees might be appointed from the different groups that constitute the citizens of the school, but they may also come from outside and be chosen because of their expertise or commitment to quality education as well as for their commitment to the values that define the school's shared educational program. A school that emphasizes health services might have some trustees who are nurses, physicians, or practicing scientists. Presumably, like the school council, members of a board of governors or trustees will view themselves as representing the entire school and will seek mechanisms that give authoritative voice to all citizens of the school.

Why include a trusteeship in this list of options when a board of trustees is an unelected body whose members may come from outside of the school community? One reason is that a trusteeship is a form of local governance that operates at the school level. Moreover, in my experience (largely in England where boards of governors are common), trustees or boards of governors are often very directly involved with the schools they govern. And they often find it easier to take an all-school view of their school and are less given to factional-ism than elected groups. They can facilitate a democratic school climate.

Which is best? Much depends on local conditions. For the most part, a combination of school councils and town meetings seems best for public schools and a trusteeship with town meetings for private schools. When a public school is quasi-private such as charter schools are, a trusteeship with town meetings may also be most appropriate. What is essential is that certain principles are respected: All members of the school polity are citizens and entitled to an authoritative voice; the relationships of loyalty and trust between the collegium and the other citizens of the school must be highly prized; and such democratic institutions as exist should not be occasions for interest group politics, but rather consensus and an all-school point of view should be emphasized.

Of course these institutions must operate within the fabric of a democratic society in which the sovereignty of the legislature remains the core meaning of democracy. If they are to be possible, legislatures must cede significant decision making authority to local schools.

A community that seeks to be both a community of practice and a democratic community must integrate the norms of governance of intellectual community and democratic community. It does this by creating a collegium where the voice of teachers is authoritative about what counts as teaching with integrity and is substantial about other educational matters. It must also create a democratic forum in which all citizens of the school can have an authoritative voice. Good governance is the result of an interaction between the collegium and a democratic forum, one rooted in loyalty and trust. This is not easy to achieve. Human beings are often contentious and selfish creatures. But this is what is called for if we wish to have schools that are both intellectual and democratic communities.

DEMOCRATIC COMMUNITIES AND COMMON GOODS

In a polity citizens are bound together by a sense of sharing a common fate and by common experiences. The polity is pervaded by a sense of WITT ("We're in this together") rather than YOYO ("You're on your own"). Democratic polities express the desire to share a common fate by creating and pursuing common goods. *Common goods* are things we pursue together, share in equally, and provide from collective resources. Their pursuit both expresses and creates community.

I can better explain the meaning of common goods by looking at a distinction between aggregative democracy and deliberative democracy (Young, 2000)and a related distinction between public goods and common goods. *Aggregative democracy,* as I use the term here, has two features: First, democracy is understood to be the means to distribute what some economists call public goods: goods not efficiently distributed by markets. Second, for aggregative democracy, the role of government in the provision of public goods is to simulate the market—that is, to satisfy the preferences that people have roughly to the degree that they have them.

On this view, the preferred way of distributing goods and services is the free market. This is the case both because the market is thought to be more efficient than other mechanisms but also because in a free society people have a right to want what they want and to use their resources in the marketplace to satisfy their wants. Markets express a kind of liberty.

However, the market is not an efficient way to distribute certain goods—sewers, highways, military forces, or even education (Friedman, 1962)—typically because these goods involve what economists call *externalities* or "neighborhood effects." These occur when the benefits of a purchase accrue to someone other than their purchaser. (See Chapter 8 for a fuller account.) When there are externalities, markets do not function well. People will not purchase as much of these goods as they desire because others may benefit without paying. Producers cannot get an adequate price for their products. Thus free transactions between producers and consumers are ineffective in securing these goods. Such goods must be provided by some other means, often by the government.

Jane Mansbridge (1980) describes aggregative democracy as a process where "voters pursue their individual interests by making demands on the political system in proportion to the intensity of their feelings" (p. 17). Aggregative democracy is thought to do this because politicians can secure reelection by satisfying their constituent's preferences. Aggregative democracy is thus an expression of YOYO rather than WITT; it sees democracy as a political mechanism where individuals pursue their own self interest in competition with others. In aggregative democracy, government institutions do not judge people's preferences. They simply try to package them so that as many people get as much of what they want as possible.

In contrast, *deliberative democracy* is a process in which citizens deliberate about the needs and interests of all and choose which goods will benefit the community as a whole. These are common goods. *Common goods* differ from public goods in the following ways. First, when we pursue common goods politically, we take the interests of others into consideration. Suppose I want a large gas-hogging SUV. I can afford to buy it, and I can afford to put gasoline into it. But I do not get an SUV because I believe that Americans need to conserve energy. When I waste gasoline, I harm my fellow citizens. Common goods are those in which others have an interest. Deliberation about common goods considers these interests. We pursue goods that are mutually beneficial.

Second, common goods take justice into account. There are some goods (e.g., health care) to which people may be entitled independently of their ability to pay for them because they are minimal conditions of a decent life. We provide (or should provide) such goods because we value all people equally. Hence we do not let some things depend on the market.

Third, common goods are achieved deliberatively by a process that requires us to critique our preferences and those of others in the light of justice and what is in all of our collective best interests. The process of deliberation is one in which all have an equal voice and the interests of all count equally.

Fourth, common goods express our desire to share a common fate and to engage in cooperation toward shared ends. Common goods are those we choose because they enable community and cooperation.

Fifth, common goods are provided from common resources.

And finally, common goods are available to all by virtue of membership in the democratic community.

When we seek to create common goods democratically, we are thus not trying to simulate the market, and we are not using the political system merely to pursue our own good. Instead we deliberate together about those goods which we will collectively pursue because they are in the best interest of all. The democratic pursuit of common goods is thus community constituting.

What are the common goods of a school that is a community? In Chapter 3 I discussed the idea that an educational community is created by having a shared educational project. Such a project involves shared educational goals, a shared language, cooperative activities in pursuit of these goals, and shared success. In a democratic school the shared educational project is viewed as the principal common good. What follows?

One thing that follows is that the success of all members of a democratic community is valued equally. The success of each is the success of all. Some shared educational projects may value the success of all because the nature of the project is such that people must succeed together or not at all. Musical organizations and sports teams are like this. Moreover, in a democratic community each individual is a potential resource for others: Students teach and learn from other students. Finally, even when these conditions do not hold, the success of any student is valued simply because that student is valued. When educational goods are the common goods of a democratic community, the success of the least able student is valued because that student is valued. Democratic communities measure their success by the success of their weakest members.

EQUAL OPPORTUNITY AND DEMOCRATIC INCLUSION

Citizens of a polity must value one another equally and treat one another justly. What does this require? The quote from *Brown v. Board of Education* that begins this chapter states that segregation was harmful because it stigmatized Black children and claims that this stigma harmed them and tainted their education.

I want to construct a reading about this passage that sees it as concerned with two distinguishable ideas about justice. The first concerns equality of educational opportunity. The second concerns what I call "communicative justice." Both are required by a democratic community.

Brown seems first of all concerned with equal educational opportunity. Chief Justice Warren who authored the opinion had already written about the fact that education had become essential to the life prospects of children in a way that had not been true previously. Schooling had become a principal instrument in acquiring the talents that are the basis of success in a market economy that depends significantly on knowledge. If so, the equal protection of the laws requires an equal education.

What is an equal education? This is a complex matter, but I begin with a simple formulation: An *equal education* is one in which neither access to education nor the outcomes of education depend on characteristics such as race, religion, ethnicity, gender, or sexual preference. This seems to be what Warren was getting at. Segregation is harmful to the education of African American students. It leads to unequal achievement and diminished life prospects. That is unjust.

Warren's account asserts a theory of how segregation produces this harm. Segregation stigmatizes Black children and this stigma is internalized as feelings of inferiority. These feelings affect learning. Because segregation itself affects education, segregated schools are inherently unequal.

A lot has happened since *Brown v. Board of Education* in 1954. Through the 1960s and 1970s the Supreme Court aggressively desegregated America's public schools. Since then they have backed off, claiming that the Constitution requires only that access to schools be color-blind, holding that neighborhood schools are permissible even when they lead to significant racial imbalance, and rejecting voluntary desegregation plans that use race as a criterion to assign pupils in order to achieve racial balance (*Parents v. Seattle,* 2007). There continue to be large differences in achievement between White and non-White students and similar disparities between income groups.

How shall we think of *Brown* now? I suggest that we find two ideas in *Brown* essential. And I suggest that we ignore one feature of *Brown.* The part of *Brown* I want to ignore is the empirical theory that connects segregation with damaged self-esteem and diminished achievement. Is this theory true? Was it true in 1954? I don't know. I have two reasons for concern: First, subsequent research has shown that there is significant association between SES and achievement (Rothstein, 2004). This has proven to be the salient issue rather than the educational consequences of stigmatizing African Americans.

A second concern is that it is problematic to make the rejection of segregated schools dependent on the consequences of segregation on educational attainment. Would we find state-imposed racial segregation acceptable if it produced no educational harm? Suppose it was even beneficial to African Americans as some states (*Stell v. Savannah*) claimed in the wake of *Brown* (Strike, 1981). Would "beneficial" segregation be OK? Surely not. What we should conclude from *Brown* is that the stigmatization of citizens is itself a harm and an injustice regardless of its consequences for equal opportunity.

Thus *Brown* has two lessons that we should cling to: First, we owe equal educational opportunity to all of our students; and, second, we should not act so as to stigmatize any students.

Let's first consider equal opportunity. John Rawls (1971) suggests that we can divide equal opportunity into two parts. The first he calls "positions open to talents." Justice requires fair hiring, and fair hiring requires that we hire people on the basis of their ability to do the job rather than on the basis of irrelevant characteristics such as race. The second part of equality of opportunity is equal educational opportunity. We owe people a fair chance to acquire the talents that are the basis of fair hiring. This requires an equal education. An equal education is one in which access and outcomes do not depend on irrelevant characteristics such as race or class. It provides for fair competition for socially valuable skills.

Fair competition is not enough for schools that seek to be democratic communities. I have suggested that democratic societies and democratic schools are to be judged by how they treat their weakest members. Rawls captures this idea by arguing that, so far as the distribution of wealth is concerned, just societies are required to maximize the welfare of the least advantaged. In education contexts, I want to put this idea in a different way.

Just and democratic schools should value all equally. Just schools must treat students in such a way as to communicate the message that all are equally valued. On my reading of *Brown* this message is put negatively. The state may not stigmatize any of its citizens. Doing so is itself an injustice regardless of the consequences of the stigma. I would prefer a more positive formulation. We must act so as to communicate the message that all are valued equally.

Consider an example: Susan is a blind child in Ms. O.'s third grade. Ms. O. wishes to fully include her in the class so far as is possible. The school is also committed to this. One consequence is that Ms. O. works hard to teach Susan to read Braille, and the school has provided special resources to this end in the form of a special teacher. Ms. O also tries to structure her lessons around materials that she can find in Braille. She has learned to read Braille herself, and she takes considerable time helping Susan.

Ms. O.'s school has physical education for third-grade students three times a week. Ms. O. has worked with the physical education teacher and with the other students to ensure that Susan can participate. Games such as dodge ball are avoided because Susan cannot play them. Relay races are frequent because Susan can participate by running with other students who hold her hand. Ms. O. has worked hard to get sighted students in her class to consider working with Susan a privilege.

Is this level of commitment to inclusion a requirement of justice? Consider an objection: Suppose Ms. O. were accused of unfairly favoring Susan. Let's view this as a claim about resource allocation. The school puts considerable additional resources into Susan's education in comparison with those provided for other children. Ms. O. devotes more of her time to Susan than to other students. Curricular activities and the activities of the physical education class are structured to accommodate Susan. Other children are presumably denied resources and opportunities as a result. They get an education that is less well adapted to their needs. Is this fair?

It might be argued that it is unfair and inefficient. Other students get less because Susan gets more. And in the long run the resources expended on these other students might have a larger impact on society's productivity. Perhaps we cannot know this. We cannot know what any of our children will become. But we can know that some children face severe limits on their capacity to be productive: For example, children with severe cognitive disabilities are unlikely to become engineers. Should we not take this into account? Should we not put our resources where they are likely to produce the most benefit? Is it not unfair to other children when we do not?

Against this we might argue that there are other benefits to be considered in addition to academic productivity. Susan's classmates, for example, are learning lessons in the humane treatment and acceptance of others. They will be better people and better citizens for that reason. This is a benefit. We must count it.

Helping students to accept others and to value others who are different from themselves is indeed a benefit, but I do not want to judge the justice of cases such as Susan's by a cost-benefit procedure. Instead, I propose that we treat such cases as matters of *communicative justice*. That is, the school must act toward Susan and toward all of its students in ways that communicate that she is valued equally with other students. This means that steps must be taken to include her. Thus what Ms. O. is doing is justified by the idea of communicative justice.

Is Ms. O. doing too much? Is there is a rule that will give a precise answer to the question as to how to strike a balance between Susan's welfare and the welfare of others? I doubt there is such a rule. No doubt we could recognize the injustice of extreme cases. If Ms. O. did nothing special for Susan, leaving her to profit as she could from education materials she could not read, we could be sure that Susan was being treated unjustly. Or if Ms. O. taught no one but Susan ignoring other students, we could conclude that other students were being treated unfairly. But Ms. O. is doing what she can to include Susan. In doing so she is expressing the fact that Susan is of equal value.

What communicative justice requires is that we take steps that reasonable people would see as expressing that Susan is valued equally with other students. We can debate whether one strategy or another is best, but I do not believe there are rules that can formally decide such cases. What we want is schools that seek to value all students equally and that express this through reasonable steps to include them.

This is what democratic schools require. We value students regardless of their ability, regardless of their background, their religion, or their culture. We show that we value them by real and substantial efforts at inclusion. We do not value them as potential productive assets. We do not see their inclusion as a form of fair competition. Instead, we show that they are valued.

DEMOCRACY, CHOICE, AND THE COMMON SCHOOL

While schools that are communities should have a common core of goals such as autonomy and citizenship, they may and perhaps should differ from each other in how they pursue these goals so long as they pursue them through authentic teaching. Core goals can be expressed through different themes. They may reflect the desire to emphasize different parts of the curriculum or different professional or vocational aspirations. Thus we may have and should encourage schools of the arts, schools that emphasize multiculturalism, or schools that focus on biotechnology. I do not believe that every school needs to have a distinctive theme or emphasis in order to be a community, but I do believe that we should provide comprehensive schools only as circumstances (such as inadequate population density) dictate or as one option in a school system in which most of the schools are more focused.

Two of the four C's of community–coherence and cohesion–suggest why. A school that attempts to be all things to all people is not likely to be either coherent or cohesive. It will have to satisfy many conflicting aspirations. It will tend to offer many electives and undermine a common experience. It will privatize goals as though it were a bank or a shopping mall.

If we consider the Common Principles of the Coalition of Essential Schools, we find additional reasons to encourage diverse orientations among different schools. Schools that are not focused on something that they distinctly pursue are not likely to do well in emphasizing depth over breadth or encouraging mastery.

Moreover, while part of the emphasis in creating schools that are communities is to overcome alienation by initiating students into worthwhile practices that transform their goals, it is also true that not every practice will fit every student. Some students will just like poetry more than math, or art more than history. So long as we find ways to succeed on the core goals of a community of practice, we should encourage a kind of diversification that permits a better fit between student preferences and the education they receive.

At the same time it is less clear that we should encourage all forms of diversification, for four (overlapping) reasons. First, some types of schools might tend to promote the "bads" of community, such as parochialism or intolerance. Second, some schools might not be fully committed to some of the core goals of any good education; for example, they might erode student autonomy. Third, some forms of diversification might be inconsistent with an equal or democratic education for all. Fourth, some types of school might not be suitably inclusive.

Religious schools and schools that thematize a distinct culture might be thought to be problematic in these ways. Why might we want such schools? Religious or ethnic schools might be especially important in overcoming the alienation of some students. Students from some faiths or cultures may find the commitments or cultural norms of schools not rooted in their own faith or culture alien or oppressive. We should recall that Native Americans were once sent to boarding schools to purge them of their culture. We have a Catholic school system today because Catholics once saw public schools as largely hostile to Catholicism and rooted in a kind of lowest-common-denominator Protestantism (Macedo, 2000). The Amish now argue that the norms of public schools are inconsistent with Amish values.

Indeed, some groups may find that an education rooted in their religion or culture is a requirement of survival. The Amish sometimes claim this (*Wisconsin v. Yoder*). This may be true of some Native American groups. Also, it may be argued that schools rooted in a faith or ethnic culture have a kind of moral coherence that is educationally important and that other schools lack. One of the things that people need to lead flourishing lives is a set of concepts that are orienting and identity-shaping. Such concepts provide direction in life and help people form coherent identities with a stable moral core. Religion and ethnic cultures are among the sources of such moral coherence. Indeed, it might be argued that schools grounded in a particular faith or culture can provide a better education because they can be sources of moral coherence.

A final argument is that including religious schools and ethnically rooted schools in the mix of schools available to children is a matter of simple fairness. All schools are grounded in some moral conceptions even if this grounding is tacit. If so, then might we not argue that an educational system that does not permit religious schools or ethnically rooted schools–or requires them to be provided and paid for privately (Arons, 1997)–is unfair? This unfairness may be particularly salient when we are thinking about creating schools that are communities since religious schools and ethnically rooted schools are often strong communities.

On the other hand, schools rooted in religion or an ethnic culture may be more likely than other schools to generate the "bads" of community. They may encourage parochialism and erode autonomy. They may encourage intolerance of other groups or promote an uncritical mythology concerning their own. Religious communities especially run the risk of being total communities.

In contrast, the kinds of communities I have emphasized, communities of practice and democratic communities, are partial communities. They provide guidance about some matters and are thick enough to promote coherence and cohesion and do the work of normation, but they are also consistent with diverse religions and cultures. If the point is to promote the goods of community without promoting the "bads," are not partial communities what is wanted?

Here I think the response is that while there are examples to be pointed to where schools rooted in a faith or in a particular ethnic culture may produce the "bads" of community, these defects are not inherent to religious or ethnic schools. Consider the difference between the Catholic schools described by Bryk, Lee, and Holland (1993) in *Catholic Schools and the Common Good* and the school described by Peshkin (1986) in *God's Choice*. The Catholic Schools described by Bryk et al. are exemplars of schools that are strong communities but which also provide a humanistic curriculum, have a strong commitment to social justice, and are intellectually open. The school described in *God's Choice*, however, is a total community. It promotes parochialism and intolerance in considerable measure and is significantly autonomy eroding.

Perhaps what is needed is a case-by-case review of such schools. Unhappily, this is difficult for religious schools. To permit some religious schools and not others is likely to be viewed by a court as unconstitutional content-based discrimination.

I am, thus, reluctant to include religious schools in the mix of schools that could be included in the diverse institutions to be provided at public expense and provided for by public policy. One could, under current law, do this only via a voucher program. I would prefer a system of public choice where the schools provided are diverse but are also created under guidelines set by public policy—more like current charter schools. (I discuss this more fully in Chapter 7.)

I am more open to schools rooted in an ethnic culture. Such schools perhaps run a risk of creating some of the "bads" of community. Some schools rooted in an ethnic culture have been accused of promoting racism, for example. At the same time there are many examples of good schools of this type, from language-immersion schools to Afrocentric schools, and there are not the same kinds of hurdles to their effective regulation as is the case with religious schools. And sometimes, as may be the case for some Native American groups, such schools are important to cultural survival. Moreover, in many urban areas population demographics often generate ethnically homogeneous schools. When this occurs, I see no reason why the culture of this group should not be given emphasis. A school that is overwhelmingly African American should be able to emphasize African American culture.

The development of tolerance and mutual respect are important goals for the education of democratic citizens. It is important that we encourage tolerance and mutual respect among citizens of different religions and ethnic groups. Arguably, these virtues are best encouraged in inclusive educational settings that are religiously and ethnically diverse. Religious schools and ethnically rooted schools are usually not religiously or ethnically diverse. Even when, like many Catholic schools, they accept significant numbers of students with other affiliations, they give preference to a particular view. Of course, no school that is a community will be diverse in every way. A school of music and art is likely to be populated by students with a particularly strong commitment to music and art. This too may lead to some measure of parochialism, but it is a different kind from that of a school whose students are largely of one ethnic group or one religion.

I would conclude that the theory of community I have developed neither requires nor precludes schools that are rooted in a shared religion or shared ethnicity. However, such schools raise a higher threshold of concern as to whether they create the "bads" of community. I would not make provision for religious schools in the public sector. Nor would I preclude private religious schools. I would make provision for ethnically rooted schools reluctantly both because ethnically homogeneous schools may be required for cultural survival and because the demography of American cities often creates schools that are ethnically homogeneous in any case.

Returning to my general argument, I believe that the schools of a democratic society need to be common schools, but they do not need to be comprehensive schools. That is, ideally they should be places where people from diverse groups meet and learn from and about one another, but they should not be places that try to be everything to everyone. Diverse interests can and should be served by different schools. This way schools can be coherent communities.

DEMOCRATIC SCHOOLS AND A SOCIAL CONTRACT

Democratic schools should express a kind of unity through diversity. All schools should be intellectual communities that serve core goals such as autonomy and citizenship. All schools should be democratic schools–democratically governed and with a democratic culture providing equal opportunity and democratic inclusion. All schools should view their program as a common good and as providing a common experience.

But these core goals and the intellectual practices that lead to them can be expressed in different ways in schools with different emphases and themes. Similarly, schools that are democratically governed can have different governance institutions and different democratic practices.

Schools that are communities and polities should be seen as rooted in a social contract. They should be constitutional democracies. Each school should, in effect, have a constitution that is the basis of the relationships in the schools, the basis of its deliberations and decision making, and the basis of the education provided. This constitution needs to cover the school's core values and educational philosophy, its educational practices and curriculum, and its governance.

The social contract should begin as a kind of charter—a contract between the district and the school. This charter should be the basis on which the district, or other governmental entity to which the school is ultimately responsible, approves the school, and it should be the primary way in which a district serves and protects the public interest in its schools. The charter is the primary mechanism of accountability. Schools are accountable to the terms of the charter and for doing well what they have promised to do. The charter enables the district to cede significant authority and to avoid eroding the autonomy of schools through numerous mandates and regulations.

Thinking of schools in this way allows schools to be communities of the like-minded. A polity is not a local participatory democracy created by a random assortment of people who happen to find themselves associated with a particular school. It is a community that begins as a community of the like-minded because they have chosen to work together to achieve shared educational values and common goods.

Part II

SMALL SCHOOLS, COMMUNITY, and SCHOOL REFORM

CHAPTER 6

Small Schools

Size or Community?

What calls the group into being–on the part of teachers as well as students–is a shared interest or concern. This interest becomes the nucleus around which a school community can be based. It's not enough to ground a community, but it's a start–as well as an acknowledgment of the obvious truth that a real community is unlikely to emerge from just any collection of human beings that chance brings together. For instance, teachers who disagree fundamentally on what education is about and what its top priorities should be cannot arrive at a very viable professional community. Youngsters who share few common interests or concerns aren't very likely to bond into a community of learners. To fail to acknowledge this (as we school people often do) is to close one's eyes to the way the world is.
–Mary Anne Raywid and Libby Oshiyama, "Musings in the Wake of Columbine: What Can Schools Do?"

Researchers observe that the effects of smallness on achievement are indirect, being mediated through other small-school features as quality of the social environment and students' sense of attachment to the school.
–Kathleen Cotton, *New Small Learning Communities*

Small schools are a big deal these days. There are numerous examples of successful small schools and a growing body of literature documenting their success. (For some useful examples see Cotton, 1996; Cotton, 2001; Howley, 2002; Lee & Smith, 1997; Meier, 2002a, 2002b; Nathan & Febey, 2001; Raywid, 1996, 1997, 1999; Toch, 2003.) There is development, enthusiasm, and money associated with their expansion. The Gates Foundation (whose enthusiasm seems to be waning recently) has gotten behind the enterprise and put substantial resources into the development of small schools. Many large urban districts–New York, Chicago, Boston, Philadelphia, Cincinnati, Minneapolis–are investing hope, effort and resources on the proposition that small schools will make their school systems better. There is particular hope that small schools are good for poor and minority students. Creating many more small schools–scaling up small–has become an important part of urban school reform.

At the same time this growing movement raises many questions. Oddly, it is unclear exactly what a "small school" is. There is no agreement about what size is optimal, and small schools often claim to be different in ways that go beyond size. Moreover, the research on small schools, while encouraging, is far from conclusive. How could it be conclusive if we are unclear as to what a small school even is? And, as the quote from Cotton above suggests, even if it seems likely that small schools do work, it is unclear why. Of course, in order to decide if some institution works, we need to be clear what it is we want it to do. If the objectives of small schools differ from those of other schools and if they have a different conception of meaningful learning, what yardstick should we use to judge them?

Answers to these questions are crucial if the small schools movement is to grow to be a real force in school reform. Raywid and Schmerler (2003) quote Rudy Crew, then chancellor of the New York City schools, as being tepid in his support of small schools because of the "question of scalability. And the only things we want to bring to scale are those things which can . . . be replicated" (p. 17). Scaling up requires clarity about what counts as doing the same thing elsewhere and about the characteristics of exemplars that led to their success. Moreover, lacking clarity about which characteristics of small schools count, it will be difficult to trust the research on them. We will not be clear what characteristics of the schools we study produce the outcomes we discover. Finally, if we are unclear about what we want when we try to scale up small schools, we are likely to use the lowest-common-denominator definition of what they are. This means that we will focus on size, and we will tend to lose whatever else is distinctive about small schools.

What is most important about small schools, I argue, is their potential to create community. Most small school advocates would agree at least with the idea that community is important. At the same time, I worry that the small schools movement lacks an adequate conception of a good educational community and that in the process of scaling up it will be easy to assume that smallness is sufficient to create educational communities.

RESEARCH ON SMALL SCHOOLS

Research on small schools can be traced back to Barker and Gump's (1964) *Big Schools, Small Schools*. Barker and Gump found that the small schools they studied in Kansas had a significant impact on the ability of students to participate in extracurricular activities and to occupy leadership roles and that these advantages improved many aspects of their education.

Research on small schools has tended to follow in the tradition of Barker and Gump in two ways. It has emphasized school size as the crucial variable, and it has seen school size as affecting the education of students largely because it has an effect on the social relationships within the school. In Barker and Gump, the crucial variable was the "understaffing" of positions in small schools and small towns requiring more involvement of students and citizens respectively. Current research, however, tends to emphasize more intimate teacher-student relationships (personalization) over opportunities for participation.

With a couple of exceptions, studies of small schools tend to produce a fairly high level of consensus about the value of small schools. (Useful reviews of this literature include Cotton, 2001; Nathan & Febey, 2001; Raywid, 1999.) Here are some of the typical and crucial claims made by small schools advocates:

- In small schools students learn more.
- Small schools have higher graduation rates.
- Small schools are especially effective for poor and minority students.
- Small schools are safer. They have fewer discipline problems.
- Small schools produce better work environments for teachers and students.
- Small schools produce a sense of community and enhance a sense of belonging.
- Small schools produce higher rates of satisfaction among teachers, parents, and students.

While the numerous studies about small schools vary considerably in quality and many are overly anecdotal, nevertheless, the consistency of these findings is impressive. This consistency leads Raywid (1999) to comment on the findings as follows:

> All of these things we have confirmed with a clarity and at a level of confidence rare in the annals of education research. As one researcher summed it up, "a large body of research in the affective and social realms overwhelmingly affirms the superiority of small schools" (Cotton, 1996). Another researcher noted that size exerts a "unique influence" on students' academic accomplishment, with a strong negative relationship linking the two: the larger the school, the lower the students' achievement levels (Howley, 1994).

This last comment may oversimplify the matter. One of the most rigorous studies of school size is "High school size: Which works best, and for whom?" by Lee and Smith (1997). This study takes a careful quantitative look at the relationship between school size and achievement in mathematics and reading. Growth in achievement was measured from the 8th to the 12th grade. The study addressed three questions: "What size school is optimal for student learning?" "How does school size affect the equitable distribution of learning?" and "Are these results the same for different types of students?"

The Lee and Smith study finds that the optimal school size for student learning is between 600 and 900 students. Moreover, in schools that are substantially larger than this range and in schools that are much smaller, there is a significant negative effect on learning. At the same time, learning outcomes are more equitably distributed in much smaller schools. The study also finds that while the 600–900 range is optimal for students of different classes and races, schools above this optimal range have a disproportionately negative effect on poor or minority students. This is particularly noteworthy because minority students are disproportionately located in large urban schools.

What is the mechanism by which school size affects learning? This question was not addressed empirically in the study, but the authors do note that

> Although our analyses support the presence of a direct link between high school size and student learning, logic argues otherwise. More likely, our findings about size represent a proxy explanation for basic features of the organization and process of high schools: the character of the curriculum, relationships among school members, and the extracurriculum. (Lee & Smith, p. 219)

These results support the main lines of argument for small schools, but they are somewhat narrow in their scope. The study does not consider the broader range of claims made by small schools advocates. For example, it does not consider graduation rates, college attendance, or citizenship. Moreover, while the study does distinguish between high- and low-minority schools, the sample contains private schools, rural schools, and urban schools, but does not distinguish them. We do not know the extent to which the public schools in the sample are rural or urban, but it is worth noting that the data relied on by the study date from 1988. Thus it is unlikely that the study picks up many of the small schools that have recently been created in urban districts. This suggests that we can generalize these results to urban small schools only on the assumption that the differences between rural and urban small schools have no significant effects on them.

Recently, several big-city school districts have invested considerable resources in small schools. Among them are Chicago and New York; both have been the beneficiary of generous funding from the Gates Foundation. Recent results from evaluation studies are less encouraging than early studies so far as achievement is concerned, and results concerning mathematics are particularly worrisome (Wyse, Keesler, & Schneider, 2008). These results are particularly important both because they are more recent than Lee and Smith's work and other studies of small schools, and also because they look at attempts by large city systems to scale up small schools.

In Chicago, researchers (Kahne, 2008; Kahne, Sporte, De la Torre, & Easton, 2008) report that students in small schools experience more "press" for academic achievement and a more supportive educational environment. Retention and graduation rates also seemed to improve. Teachers are more collegial and committed. However, there was no significant improvement in achievement in mathematics and reading. When race and SES were controlled for, outcomes comparing students attending small schools and comprehensive high schools were nearly identical. These researchers also suggest that there were few changes in the character of instruction in these schools.

Other studies of schools that were funded through Gates Foundation grants show mixed achievement outcomes (Mitchell et al., 2005; Rhodes et al., 2005; see also Quint, 2006). Rhodes et al. (2005) summarize the results of their evaluations as follows:

- Teachers and students at both newly established and redesigned schools are making progress in developing a positive culture that supports student learning.
- Compared to comprehensive high schools, the quality of student work in new and redesigned high schools is higher in English/language arts, but slightly lower in mathematics.
- Initial student achievement levels are promising for English/language arts, but not for mathematics. (pp. 2, 3)

What shall we make of these studies? Diane Ravitch (2008) in an online commentary entitled *Bill Gates and His Silver Bullet* provides a rather negative assessment:

> The bad news about the Gates' initiative began to accumulate in 2005, when a Gates-funded study by the American Institutes for Research showed that students in traditional, comprehensive high schools were learning more mathematics than those in the Gates' small schools. The researchers also found that "relevance" was not correlated with the quality of student learning. Then in 2006, additional research commissioned by the foundation concluded that the Gates-funded small schools had "higher attendance rates but lower test scores" than other high schools within the same school districts in both reading and mathematics.

Ravitch also attributes the reported higher retention and graduation rates of Gates-funded New York City schools to the fact that these schools were able to exclude special-needs and limited-English children.

Ravitch's assessment seems overly negative. In a 1996 review of research on small schools Cotton (1996) has more positive comments:

> About half the student achievement research finds no difference between the achievement levels of students in large and small schools. . . . The other half finds student achievement in small schools to be superior to that in large schools. . . . None of the research finds large schools superior to small schools in their achievement effects. Consequently, we may safely say that student achievement in small schools is at least equal–and often superior–to student achievement in large schools. Achievement measures used in the research include school grades, test scores, honor roll membership, subject-area achievement, and assessment of higher order thinking skills.

Even given the results Ravitch discusses, Cotton's comments seem a better assessment of the overall picture. While the Gates results do indicate that there have been some negative results, nevertheless they essentially suggest that the effects on achievement in these cases are largely neutral. This is not altogether a ringing endorsement of small schools. However, these studies also note that these schools are new. Any major reform requires a fairly long shakedown cruise before evaluation results can be viewed as authoritative. Thus the results of these studies are hardly conclusive. Perhaps we may reasonably conclude that small schools are no silver bullet, but the suggestion that they were supposed to be a silver bullet belongs to Ravitch. What we should conclude is that small schools are a project under development that has shown some promising results and that their development will require time, effort, and deliberation about what works and what does not.

These studies do suggest an improved educational climate for teachers and students. This is a positive matter regardless of effects on achievement. We should, certainly, value the quality of life of students and teachers in schools apart from achievement scores; schools are not boot camps. That more students graduate (at least in Chicago and in most other places) is also good news. After all, the effects on life prospects of education flow from school completion as well as from what one learns. Moreover, it seems quite likely that students who stay in school learn more than if they had dropped out–a fact perhaps not adequately considered in studies that tend to compare students who remain in different sorts of schools.

Finally, we need to consider that the educational outcomes on which some of these evaluations focus are largely confined to reading and mathematics as measured by standardized tests. We do not know much about the broader goals of these schools, whether goals other than those measures were achieved, or about any possible trade-offs that might have been involved among measured outcomes and other goals. Was a little math traded for more citizenship? We don't know.

These studies suggest that very little about instruction changed. Moreover, the improved collegiality experienced by teachers did not translate into collective effort at instructional improvement. Kahne et al. (2008) comments:

> Consistent with this perspective, a recent synthesis of MDRC studies (Quint, 2006) found that teachers in small schools reported that they lacked both the skills and the time to create their own curriculum and to integrate curricular themes of small schools into their teaching. Indeed, most teacher meetings in the small learning communities of study did not focus on instruction but rather on discipline issues, individual students' personal or academic problems, or planned small learning community field trips or parties. (p. 295)

This comment raises an important question concerning the nature of the reforms in these districts. It suggests that the teachers who participated in these new small schools were expected to alter their instructional practice, but that often there were few expectations or shared understandings about how they were to alter them. Moreover the conditions that might have enabled them to alter their instruction (training and time) were not readily available. The suggestion seems almost to be that some districts have created their small schools on the assumption that once schools are downsized, teachers will automatically have a better, more supportive, and more collegial work environment and things will happen differently in the classroom more or less as a matter of course and without additional support, planning time, or training.

If this is true, it suggests that part of the difficulty is that the effort to create small schools is not always adequately informed by a vision of the pedagogical changes that are required for small schools or the time to adequately implement them. If so, this is a narrow vision of small schools and their role in educational reform. It does not envision small schools as strong educational communities. I want to address this issue via a discussion of the question, What is a small school?

WHAT IS A SMALL SCHOOL?

One fault line concerning small schools is the difference between rural and urban small schools. I live in a very small town in New York State's Adirondack Park, the Town of Webb (TOW). Despite the fact that in area it is the largest town in the state, its total population is about 2,000. The village of Old Forge, the "population center," has about 1,200 people. The TOW school district teaches about 350 students K–12. In order to get to this number it takes high school students from two adjoining school districts so small that they are unable to operate a high school.

The town and the school are paradigmatic of communities of place. The TOW school is an important center of community life and community identity. Participation in extracurricular events is very high. Here students are involved and cared for more or less as a matter of course. They rarely "fall between the cracks." If there is a place in America where the idea that it takes a whole village to raise a child is practiced, this is it. But the village takes little thought about this. It just happens.

Despite the fact that the TOW is not a wealthy place (family income is about $10,000 below the state average) students in the TOW school do well on state tests. Almost all students are at least proficient on No Child Left Behind tests. Almost all students pass the New York State Regents exams. And almost all students graduate and go on to college. If one wanted a poster child to advertise the claim that small schools do well by their students, the TOW School would qualify. It typifies many of the favorable qualities that Barker and Gump found in *Big Schools, Small Schools*, qualities that make them good places for kids.

While the small schools movement might be thought to have begun with rural schools, it is far from clear that the TOW school is a small school as that is now often understood. This school and other rural schools are different from urban small schools in so many ways that it is hazardous to generalize from research on schools that are naturally small to the small schools that are created in urban areas.

The TOW school is a community of place. Most urban small schools must create community from a group of strangers, often diverse strangers. If they are to be communities, they will have to create a community of purpose where there is none.

The TOW school does not struggle with bureaucracy. The district is so small that it would be difficult for it to create one. Students, teachers, and administrators interact in multiple ways. In urban small schools keeping the bureaucracy at bay is a constant preoccupation.

The TOW school does not struggle with diversity. There is little diversity to struggle with. The student body of most urban small schools is diverse (or largely poor and minority) and that is a fact that must be taken into account.

What urban and rural small schools do have in common is small size. Even here there are differences. In rural areas the size of a school results from community demography. In urban areas it may be chosen. And there is not, among small schools advocates, agreement about what size is optimal. Many resist the idea that we should define small schools by a number attained by looking at the relations between size and achievement. (Raywid & Osiyama, 2000) give a qualitative and functional characterization:

What do high schools need to be . . . ? Small enough so that people can know one another. Small enough so that individuals are missed when they are absent. Small enough so that the participation of all students is needed. Small enough to permit considerable overlap in the rosters from one class to another. Small enough so that the full faculty can sit around a table together and discuss serious questions. Small enough to permit the flexibility essential to institutional responsiveness–to the special needs of individuals and to the diverse ways teachers want to teach. (p. 446)

Small schools also often have distinct organizational forms. Tom Vander Ark (2002), in an article entitled "Personalization: Making Every School a Small School," talks about a continuum of small learning communities that "includes houses, academies, schools-within-a-school, and small autonomous schools." These different types of enterprises are often lumped together as small schools.

Many small schools are themed. They may be schools of the arts or of science or of technology. They may have names like High Tech High, School of Environmental Studies, Parkland Magnet MS for Aerospace Technology, or Arizona Agribusiness and Equine Center (Nathan & Febey, 2001). In some works about small schools the thematic character of these schools seems essential. Toch's (2003) book *High Schools on a Human Scale* places considerable emphasis on the idea of focus:

The best schools have a clear sense of what they hope to achieve with their students. They are "focused." Their curricula, their teaching strategies, the way they organize their school day, even, in many instances, the design of their buildings, are aligned with their educational aims. (p. 13)

Some of the schools he discusses have distinct pedagogical approaches. Small schools sometimes aspire to be democratic schools (Apple & Beane, 1995). Themed schools, schools built around the assumptions of the Coalition of Essential Schools, and schools that emphasize authentic teaching and learning and assessment by performance and portfolio suggest that small schools are not just about size. They are often associated with distinct goals and distinct views of pedagogy and curriculum.

In these developments we have an expansion of the idea of a small school, one that makes urban small schools different from rural ones, and we have the beginnings of potentially competing theories about what is central. A minimalist view of small schools emphasizes size. But even here it is no longer clear that size has to do altogether with the number of students in a building. It may have more to do with the pattern of interaction between adults and students.

For others what is important is personalization. Still others talk about focus or about particular ways of teaching and evaluation. And, of course, another view is that the small schools movement is about creating good educational communities united by a shared conception of a good education. Smallness is a step on the way.

So what is a small school? This brief tour through some different conceptions suggests four different answers depending on the features we emphasize:

1. Small schools are schools that have fewer than a certain number of students.
2. Small schools have certain social characteristics. They are small enough so that everyone knows everyone else or so that the staff can meet in one room. They are personalized.
3. Small schools have certain organizational characteristics. They are autonomous. They are not bureaucratic. They are flexible. They can be responsive to individual needs. They are collegial. They are more coherent or more focused. They are less likely to have significant tracking and will have fewer electives. They may have distinct forms of governance.
4. Small schools have distinctive educational programs. They may be themed, they may follow the Common Principles of the Coalition of Essential Schools, they may emphasize portfolio evaluations of student work, or they may have some other educational approach that distinguishes them from standard public schools.

These characteristics are interdependent. One might view them as a kind of developmental hierarchy where the higher "stages" depend on the lower ones. Consider some comments by Cotton (2001):

> What small size does is to provide an optimal setting for high-quality schooling to take place. It facilitates the use of organizational arrangements and instructional methods that lead to a more positive school climate and higher student learning. Experienced practitioners and knowledgeable researchers have much to say about the conditions and practices that can enable small schools to achieve their potential to become true learning communities. (p. 21)

Here the four characteristics of small schools are linked. Size provides a context for where the higher stages of my developmental hierarchy are possible, but it is not viewed as a sufficient condition for attaining them. Kahne's discussion of small schools in Chicago suggests that many of those small schools were stuck somewhere between the second and third stages. Small size has created a more supportive environment, but this has not translated into meetings focused on instruction or into significant instructional change. The description of the creation of these small schools suggests that they were supposed to create working environments for teachers that would be more supportive and collegial. This in turn was supposed to lead to instructional innovation and improvement. However, it is not clear that there was a particular vision of the character of that improvement. It almost seems that the message was that, if we improve the climate for teachers, they will come up with better ways to teach. The start-up hypothesis seems to be "If we create small schools, something good will happen."

As suggested, we might view these four features of small schools via an analogy with stage theories in the sense that the lower stages are often preconditions of the higher ones. They are stages of organizational dependency in the ongoing life of a school. The ability to implement the higher stages depends on the lower, but this is not a reason to believe that creating a small school is a sufficient condition for achieving the higher stages.

If it is not, then it is important to the process of creating schools that are genuinely innovative as well as good educational communities that the vision for the educational program comes first. Otherwise what we are likely to create is conventional schools with fewer students. Consider that most of the exemplars of small schools from which the small schools movement draws its inspiration (Meier, 2002a; Nathan & Febey, 2001; Toch, 2003) were created by people with a vision of a good education, not just a vision for smallness. In school reform, a vision of "just small" is a small vision.

It is thus important that we think of smallness and personalization as the preconditions of a good educational community rather than as sufficient for community. Community is more than a network of warm personal relationships; it is people united by shared educational purpose toward which there is common effort. It is common goods democratically pursued. Remembering this helps understand why the vision must come first. If it does not, then we will be inclined to think that in creating a small personalized environment we have created a community. And that will tempt us to think that the vision can wait.

There are other ways in which what counts as a small school can be ambiguous. One is that there are differences in what I call "school implementation structures." Some small schools are embedded within schools-within-a-school arrangements. As Vander Ark (2002) notes, there is a continuum of small learning communities in addition to free standing autonomous schools. These include "house" plans that group students in durable "houses" for some noncurricular purposes to schools within a school where schools with varying degrees of independence share a common building and may pool some resources or activities such as athletics or AP courses. Do these different implementation structures make a difference? Lee and Ready (2007) suggest they do. Nathan and Febey (2001) along with Lee and Ready suggest that schools within a school are less successful than stand-alone schools.

Another set of issues flows from the fact that the small schools movement has an ambiguous relationship to other types of school reform efforts. How are we to see the relationship of the small schools movement to choice or to charter schools? Most charter schools are small if one uses a numerical definition, and some writers on small schools (Nathan & Febey, 2001) include charter schools among their examples of small schools. At the same time, a standard justification of charter schools is that they produce quasi markets that introduce competition into education (Hoxby & Murarka, 2007). Charter school advocates often view competition as the mechanism that creates successful charter schools. Small schools advocates rarely mention this as a possibility. They bring different theories to the school reform table, but apply them to an overlapping set of institutions.

A final point is that in many ways small schools are quite diverse in their themes and approaches. Consider some additional small schools discussed in Nathan and Febey (2001): Academy Charter School uses the Core Knowledge Curriculum developed by Hirsch (1987); Alpha High School emphasizes the world of work and career exploration; New County School is teacher organized and run as a workers co-op. For some schools the name itself indicates what is distinctive about the school. These include Clark Montessori, Mesa Arts Academy, and El Puente Academy for Peace and Justice. Some of these schools are charter schools, some are schools within schools, some focus on serving minority populations, and some work with at-risk populations. There is a remarkable diversity of institutional types, curricular emphases, and educational philosophies.

What do they have in common? Perhaps Rudy Crew is right. If the answer to the question "What is a small school?" is "Let a thousand flowers bloom," then each small school will be different from all the rest and we will only be able to judge each school by its own purposes. If so, this is likely to frustrate policy makers no end. It is difficult to scale up uniqueness, and it is difficult for states to assess schools with divergent aims and curricula. If we cannot do this, how are legitimate public interests and the welfare of children to be protected? Indeed, in what do they consist?

How are we to get a tighter definition of what a small school is? How will we address Crew's concern? One way is to claim that what small schools have in common is that they are small and to argue that smallness itself accounts for their success. If so, all we need to do is scale up small. What could be simpler?

But this response foregoes much of what is important about small schools and sacrifices their potential as a distinctive vision of school reform. It assumes that if we create schools that are small something good will happen. It also creates some puzzlement as to how we will understand success or failure. Raywid (1996), comments on a failed small school:

> With such piecemeal and partial implementation . . . there were minimal improvements in student performance and virtually no gains in authentic achievement, equity, empowerment, the establishment of a learning community, the stimulation of reflective dialogue, or accountability. (p. 36)

Consider that, if we think size is the defining characteristic of small schools, Raywid's analysis of failure makes little sense. On a "size only" account what is there to fail to implement? We need only have fewer students. Raywid's comments assume that there is more to a small school than size. It was the failure to implement a distinctive program that accounted for failure. We need a more robust account.

The account we need should provide a distinctive vision of school reform. As small schools move up through my hierarchy of four defining characteristics, as they become less about size and more about such things as authentic teaching, portfolio evaluation, and themed curricula, small schools becomes less about a "technique" for school improvement and more about a "paradigm" for school reform.

Techniques are practices that can be put to use in meeting a wide range of goals and can be employed by people with different core conceptions of school reform. If phonics is the best way to teach reading, it is the best way to teach reading regardless of whether one believes in choice or in systemic reform as the basic model of school reform. But when the small schools movement begins to talk about alienation and personalization and to link these notions not only to size but also to views about institutional forms and governance and views of instruction and assessment, small schools advocates are moving beyond the recommendation of educational techniques and toward a vision of school reform that may be at odds with other views.

Ultimately, I think the answer to Rudy Crew's concern about scalability is to focus on the idea that small schools are communities. This view requires a viable conception of community. Small school advocates seem mostly to agree that community is important but do not always have much clarity about what a good educational community is.

SMALL SCHOOLS, PERSONALIZATION, AND COMMUNITY

In the preface of this book I suggested that its themes could be summarized by three aphorisms:

Authentic learning is an act of affiliation.
We are all in this together.
Alienation is the problem; community is the cure.

What is the core of the small schools movement? What provides for unity in diversity? I would propose that the core problem that small school advocates have identified (or should identify) is student alienation and disengagement. The core solution is community. Many of the concepts that have distinguished the discourse of small school advocates can best be formulated in the context of the idea that small schools aim to cure alienation through community.

An emphasis on alienation seems quite consonant with what small school advocates have said about their point. Consider the following comments in Wasley et al. (2000):

> Why create small schools? Above all, in order to address four specific problems: to create small, intimate learning communities where students are well known and can be pushed and encouraged by adults who care for and about them; to reduce the isolation that too often seeds alienation and violence; to reduce the devastating discrepancies in the achievement gap that plague poorer children and, too often, children of color; and to encourage teachers to use their intelligence and their experience to help students succeed. (p. 2)

While four problems are identified and alienation is mentioned specifically in only one, overcoming student alienation seems central to each. Why talk about alienation and disengagement? The key insight is that schooling is often ineffective, not so much because the curriculum is poor or because teachers are poorly trained or inadequately "incentivized" (although all of these may be true), but because students simply do not care about mastering the curriculum that adults have put before them. They do not care because the schools they attend are large, impersonal, and bureaucratic and because the cultures and communities in which they have been raised often do not affirm the worth of the education they are provided except in instrumental ways. While educators can do little to cure the culture, they can take steps to reduce alienation in schools. Often students do not feel cared for, affirmed, or valued by adults they meet in the schools they attend. They find belonging in sub-groups–various youth cultures–or they simply are lonely. These sub-cultures are sometimes oppositional to the goals of the school. When students do not feel valued or cared for and attach themselves to oppositional groups, they are likely to respond to the school's efforts with passive resistance and occasionally active hostility. This is essentially a story about alienation. Students see the school as an alien institution that imposes its will and its values on them. They are in it, but not of it. They do not share its goals. They can affirm their worth and their value only by resistance.

What is the cure? I quote (again) a passage by Deborah Meier (2000) that I think captures the zeitgeist of the small schools movement:

> We need to surround kids with adults who know and care for our children, who have opinions and are accustomed to expressing them publicly, and who know how to reach reasonable collective decisions in the face of disagreement. That means increasing local decision making, and simultaneously decreasing the size and bureaucratic complexity of schools. (p. 20)

Let me parse this. It says (as I would like to read it):

1. Kids are alienated from the kinds of schools we now have because they are impersonal and bureaucratic.
2. We need to create schools that are communities to which kids feel they belong and whose purposes they share.
3. Schools need to be communities of two sorts:
   a. Intellectual communities where ideas are valued and discussed.
   b. Democratic communities where decision making occurs through wide participation and reasoned discussion that aims at consensus.
4. If we are to have schools like this, they must be more personal and caring, smaller, and less bureaucratic, and have more autonomy. These are the conditions that abet the formation of good school communities. To realize their potential we need a conception of good education.

Here I have cast a core theory for small schools in a way that reflects the analysis of community in Part I. It places emphasis on the kind of community we want to create rather than on the interpersonal relations educators should have with students. It sees community as the cure for alienation. Not that it devalues good personal relationships. Instead, it emphasizes their role in creating a certain form of school community as well as the role of community in creating good social relations.

This "communitarian" formulation can be juxtaposed with a more individualistic conception that sees strong personal relationships with students as important in a way that tends to disassociate these relationships from their role in creating good educational communities. The individualistic conception seeks to educate students one at a time but does not have its own conception of what makes a good education nor seeks to initiate students into a community defined by a clear conception of intellectual or democratic goals.

Consider two comments from the Small Schools Project (2009) Web site:

Small schools foster personalized learning environments where all students are known well. In small schools, students develop sustained relationships with teachers and other caring adults.

They [small schools] are personal. Every student is known by more than one adult, and every student has an advisor/advocate who works closely with her and her family to plan a personalized program. Student-family-advisor relationships are sustained over several years.

In these statements personalization seems conceived in terms of one-on-one relationships between teacher and student. (This is not true in other parts of the Web site.) Sometimes it seems to have to do as much with individualized instruction (Jenkins & Keefe, 2002) as it does with care although surely care is more central. Consider how these comments might be expressed as a theory about small schools:

1. Students will perform better and behave better when they feel cared for by adults.
2. Students will feel cared for by adults when each student is able to establish durable and desirable relationships with one or more caring adults.
3. These durable relationships permit the development of an individualized program for each student.
4. To achieve this we need to personalize the school.
5. The key to personalizing the school is small size.

I have some reservations about this overly individualistic conception of personalization. It tends to see the cure for alienation as establishing caring relationships, but it constructs these relations as one-on-one connections between students and teachers and disconnects them from belonging to or membership in an educational community. Moreover, the emphasis on individualized educational programs might be understood in a way that undermines the idea of a shared educational program and fractures the shared experience that is central to community building.

Insofar as the individualistic view of personalization has an implicit conception of community, it tends to understand community as constituted by a network of good personal relations among those who inhabit a common space rather than seeing community as being constituted by shared educational purposes and projects. When these individualized personal relationships are in the service of the development of highly individualized educational programs, they may further erode the achievement of a shared educational project.

Why is this distinction between an individualistic and a communitarian view of personalization important? In Deborah Meier's comments quoted above, the notion of personalization is linked to a picture of a good educational community. Educational goals (developing the intellect and democratic character) are constitutive of these communities.

Of course we want good individual relationships between students and teachers. But we also want those relationships to be transformative so that students come to see themselves as members of a community aiming at goals they share. And, as teachers, we want more than that students will not be alienated from us as individuals. We want them to share our purposes—to become engaged with the shared educational project of the school.

Identifying a community with a network of caring relationships has an impoverished view of the role of care in creating community. As I argued in Chapter 3, there is a "dialectical" relationship between caring and community. People, particularly young people, come to share the values and commitments of people who care for them. As they internalize the values and commitments of those who care for them, they come to see others with the same values and commitments as members of their community and to identify with and care about them for this reason. Moreover, they are able to join with these others in the pursuit of common goods that they value. Friendships are formed from these shared pursuits. Trust is established because others are cared about and because others are seen as sharing goals.

A particular kind of caring is required. It is the kind of caring that invites students into community by sharing with them things that adults have come to experience as genuinely good. It is the kind of care that promotes initiation into practices. Initiation into practices requires trust. Trust requires that teachers are seen as caring about both their subject and their students.

The mastery of practices is transformative. And this transformation is the key to overcoming alienation in an educationally relevant way. It is not just that students feel cared for. In addition, they come to experience the school's goals as their own.

For a communitarian view of personalization, caring is not just a technique. It cannot be put to the service of any form of education. It requires a view of education that seeks to create communities of practice and democratic communities by sharing with students the value of the goods internal to these forms of community. But an individualized conception of personalization disconnects care from the creation of strong educational communities and makes it into a mere technique.

If we think about small schools as attempting to create good and strong educational communities, then they are not just about size. They are about personalization, themed curricula, portfolios, authentic instruction, coaching, choice, autonomy, and much else. At their core they are about creating intellectual and democratic communities, and these other features find their point in the way they help to create such communities. Many of the apparently diffuse ideas that have attached themselves to the small schools movement can be understood as part of a coherent whole if this communitarian conception is emphasized. In contrast, an individualized conception of personalization will ultimately lead to the view that small schools are merely a technique and that much of what is important to small schools advocates about providing a good and nonalienating education is not essential.

This communitarian conception of small schools may assist in scaling up by making it possible to provide an answer to the question, "What is essential to a school being a small school?" The answer can emphasize the requirements of creating nonalienating intellectual and democratic communities. Schools that have different themes and different organizational structures can, nevertheless, be instances of the same thing.

We do not yet know whether the small schools movement can be easily scaled up. But as we try to do so, the small schools movement will inevitably rub up against the realities of urban school systems. There will be failures and frustrations. If we do not have an adequate conception of what we are trying to accomplish, we run the danger that the distinctiveness of small schools will be lost and the failures viewed as fatal to the movement. We may want to say that failures are to be attributed to the fact that the core ideas were not adequately carried out; but we cannot say this if we lack a clear view of what these ideas are. School reform is littered with undertheorized efforts abandoned before we finished a reasonable shakedown cruise. Without a coherent theory we cannot even know the degree to which we have adequately implemented what we had in mind since we had nothing clearly in mind to guide implementation. And we learn nothing from our successes or failures.

CHAPTER 7

Policies for Small Schools

Scaling Up, Keeping On

We Americans are caught in a dilemma: On the one hand, we know school reform is necessary if today's schools are going to work for today's school population, and thus we seek reform. Small schools, therefore, are intended to do more than just replicate the status quo on a smaller scale. The successful ones involve changes in curricular organization, instructional strategy, the organization of teachers' work, school culture, school and student assessment, and more. But an unresolved dilemma emerges: The people who undertake such changes by launching smaller schools find that these schools no longer fit in the very systems that were calling upon them to reform!
–Mary Anne Raywid and Gil Schmerler, *Not So Easy Going: The Policy Environment of Small Urban Schools and Schools-Within-Schools*

The vision of school reform I have been sketching requires significant changes in our educational system. These changes are difficult. They are, I believe, especially difficult in those areas where school reform is most important–in urban areas where schools are charged to educate populations with significant numbers of poor and minority children.

In many urban areas school reform faces entrenched and unresponsive bureaucracies, uncooperative unions, self-interested and occasionally corrupt politicians, frequent leadership changes and the unstable priorities that accompany them, and a fair amount of chaos, confusion, and complexity. There is no silver bullet for complexity (McQuillan, 2008) or human perversity. But clarity of purposes can help. What follows is an attempt to develop some elements of a policy framework for small schools in large districts.

If small schools that are strong communities are to have a real and enduring impact on American education, they must do more than get small and hope something good will happen. They need to be created with a vision of good educating–one that changes what goes on in the classroom, one that establishes a shared educational project that enables building a strong community. They need to be strong communities. If this is to happen, they need to begin well, and they need a supportive and stable policy environment so that they can succeed over the long haul. Beginning well and succeeding over the long haul–related but different matters–both require clarity about the changes we are trying to put in place.

In Chapter 6 I argued that we can arrange various definitions of small schools in a kind of developmental hierarchy. At the bottom is a definition emphasizing size: A small school is one with few students. Next is a definition emphasizing the quality of relationships in the school: Small schools are personalized. Third is a definition emphasizing organizational structure: Small schools are informal and collegial; they run more on trust and moral authority than on rules and compliance. Fourth, small schools have a distinctive educational program: They may be themed. They practice authentic teaching. They try to follow the Common Principles of the Coalition of Essential Schools.

If we want to have small schools that are strong communities, we need policies that will help us create schools that succeed at each level of this hierarchy at their inception. We cannot simply downsize schools and hope that the staff in the new school will find a way to climb the ladder that this hierarchy suggests. Often the ladder doesn't get climbed very far. Teachers who do not share any uniting vision are thrown together and asked to create a small school. There is little or no professional development and inadequate time to prepare. There is a poorly conceived view of the education to be provided. Obstacles may be placed in the way. Districts may be obsessed with test-based accountability. They may insist on a districtwide curriculum. Teachers may be asked to create schools where there is an emphasis on authentic teaching, but find themselves accountable for meeting benchmarks that do not measure the kinds of mastery that authentic teaching aims at.

Starting at the bottom by downsizing and asking teachers who happen to find themselves in a new small school to climb the ladder ignores the lesson of how many of the exemplars of successful small schools began. They were typically created by people with a vision, people who found ways to get districts to support their vision and who attracted like-minded people to help them carry though their vision.

Given this, how shall we scale up and how shall we continue on?

SCALING UP: PRINCIPLES FOR CREATING SUCCESSFUL SMALL SCHOOLS

No doubt there are numerous ways to scale up small schools, many of which will depend on local circumstances. Here, I argue that the best ways of scaling up will have (minimally) three features: (1) Small schools that are strong communities are created by contract; (2) they will have adequate time and resources for planning and training; and (3) they will provide for ways that those who have already created good small schools can work with those who are starting out. "Contract, Plan, Network" should be our mantra.

Two Ways to Create Small Schools

Suppose we have two large school districts both of which seek to create small schools. Let us call them Modus and Operandi. Modus and Operandi are not intended as descriptions of any real startups. (For some real examples, see Nathan, 2008; Shear et al., 2008; for discussion, see Cotton, 2006.) Their characterization is rather intended to suggest some hypotheses about the requirements of developing successful new small schools.

In the first example, Modus district officials are persuaded by various educational experts and a foundation that is interested in school reform that small schools are a good idea. The district, after some consultation with the teachers union and other stakeholders, commits to creating a number of small high schools. They decide to do this by breaking up some of their larger schools into smaller ones. These schools are selected because they are not good schools. They are characterized by low test scores, low graduation rates, considerable absenteeism and violence, and staff demoralization.

In some cases Modus will break these schools into schools within schools. In other cases there will be stand-alone schools. These decisions are made in part for logistical reasons and in part because the sponsoring foundation wishes to research these differences.

Modus decides that these schools will be staffed largely by the faculty at the schools that are to be broken up. The basic process is this: Teachers in these schools will be told that their school is to be broken up. They will be asked if they wish to teach in one of the new schools. Those who agree will choose a planning team. Those who do not will be offered a transfer. The main task of the planning team will be to determine the character of the set of new small schools resulting from the closure of their school. Each old school will be broken up into four to six new small schools depending on the number of students in the school to be closed. Each new school may have a theme or an emphasis so long as the mix of new schools is able to accommodate all of the students who are currently in the old school. The plans for each set of new schools will have to be recommended by the planning team.

Once the basic plan for these new schools is accepted, teachers who have chosen to teach in the new small schools will be allowed to opt into one of the schools recommended by their planning team. In case the numbers do not work out right, there will be a lottery.

Teachers who are not currently in the schools to be closed will be given the opportunity to opt into one of these new schools if they are not fully staffed.

The transfer of teachers into and out of the new schools will have to be balanced. The principal and assistant principals from the old school will be principals in the new schools. Additional principals will be chosen from current teachers with administrative certification.

Once the themes of the new schools are determined and the staffing worked out, new planning teams to do the detailed planning of each new school will be chosen from those teachers who selected it. Planning will be led by the new principal.

The process of creating the theme of these new schools and working out the staffing arrangements will take place during one academic year. Teachers who are on planning teams will be given a course reduction. Detailed plans for the new schools will be developed over the summer. Teachers with planning duties will be paid. Other teachers will be notified of their new responsibilities by mid-July so that they can prepare for the new school year. The district promises additional professional development in the early years of implementation.

Students who will attend these new schools will come from the schools to be closed. Each student will be asked to choose one of the new schools. If some schools are oversubscribed, there will be a lottery. Some students will get their second choice.

In the second example, Operandi similarly begins with the assistance of a foundation, a belief that small schools are a promising line of reform, and with discussions with the teachers union and other stakeholders. But in other respects it proceeds in a different way.

Operandi decides to create small schools without immediately closing any large schools. Small schools will be added gradually. The district will begin with a few schools and add more as success and demand warrant. Larger schools will be closed or consolidated as small schools take on a larger share of the district's students.

Operandi does not see the creation of small schools as a way to replace poorly performing schools or as targeted to at-risk students. It sees them as suitable for all students and available to all students in the district. It does, however, decide to make it easier for students from its more poorly performing schools to attend by locating its new small schools in the catchment areas of these schools. It hopes that the need to retain their current students will provide some incentive for poorly performing schools to improve.

Small schools would be created through an application process where teachers interested in starting a small school submit a proposal to a committee set up by the Operandi board to vet these proposals and to assist those whose proposals were accepted to create their schools. The founders of the new schools will first hire a principal who might be one of the founding teachers, and the founders and the new principal will flesh out the plan for the school and hire its teachers. So that Operandi does not have to hire a lot of new teachers, initially new schools will be staffed largely from teachers currently employed by the district who are interested in teaching in the new schools and who are acceptable to the founding teachers, but eventually these schools will be free to hire their own teachers so long as new teachers are certified. There will be a year following the acceptance of the proposal and prior to the opening of a new school for the founders and the new principal to plan, and once a staff is hired there will be time for them to participate in the planning and for professional development. As more new schools are added, older, successful small schools will participate in assisting new schools. Eventually schools will be organized into clusters, and, as the number of small schools increases, the number of clusters would expand. Clusters will provide the opportunity to network about successful strategies. Operandi hopes that the evolution of the district with a mix of small schools and larger comprehensive schools will occur gradually and will go as far as demand justifies.

It is important to understand the point of these descriptions. They are not presented as blueprints to be fleshed out in figuring out how to scale up. They are instead focused on a problem. The point of creating small schools is not just to have smaller schools, as though smallness itself is a kind of magic elixir for educational woes. It is to create small schools that are strong educational communities. But if this is what we want, we need a process to plan for such schools. We are unlikely to get them if we simply downsize and hope something good will happen.

Thus the first question we must ask about scaling up is not "How can we create small schools?" It is "How can we create small schools that are strong communities in that they begin with all of the elements a strong community requires?"

Evaluating Differences in Startup Procedures

Consider how Modus and Operandi differ. In Modus, small schools are created by breaking up large ones. New schools must accommodate all of the old school's students, and the initial plan for the mix of new schools will be created by a team of individuals chosen by teachers from the old school who wish to teach in the new small schools rather than accept a transfer. This means that while the teachers who will staff the new schools are chosen because of a preference to teach in a small school, they are not chosen because they have a commitment to any particular vision of a good education. These people have, at best, a weak commitment to a vague idea of a small school. They may also bring with them a culture of failure.

The initial planning team that is to create the mix of schools that will replace the large high school is chosen from this group. They are not asked to develop a school with a shared educational project in which they all believe. They are asked to create a differentiated set of schools that can accommodate all of the students in the school to be closed. This poses some risks. One that I will discuss later is that the new set of schools will create or re-create a tracking system among the set of new schools. But here the real risk is that these schools are not created because someone wants them and values the kind of education they propose to offer. They are created because the task is to invent differentiated small schools within a narrow range of possibilities. And those who choose them–teachers and students–must choose one school from a short list. For some the option chosen may be exactly what they want or need, but for others the choice may be the least bad alternative. This variable commitment may lead to reduced coherence in the conception of the schools created. It will be easier to settle for a weaker view of a school community.

The risk then is that these schools may be developed and then populated by people who are less than committed to the conception of a good education the school they choose represents. An additional risk is that these new schools may import the culture of failure and discouragement from the school to be closed.

Operandi's process permits a broader range of options for new schools to be proposed as well as options that begin as stronger more coherent communities. In Operandi, teachers are asked to propose schools with other like-minded teachers. What can be proposed is not constrained by the need to include everyone from a school to be closed. Once a proposal is accepted, other teachers join the staff because they share the conception of a good education proposed. The new school is planned by those with a reasonable degree of antecedent commitment and agreement to a shared educational project. Those who join later–students and teachers–join because they are committed to the new school's shared educational project.

A second difference between Modus and Operandi is the amount of planning time and the amount of professional development provided. In Operandi it is anticipated that teachers will need to make significant changes to their curriculum so as to integrate their lessons into a theme and that they will be engaged in more team teaching and integration of subject matter. History will be woven together with language studies, mathematics with science. Planning these things, it is recognized, takes time–time for teachers to discuss, study, and learn to work together.

A third difference is the patterns of association that are likely to develop among the teachers in different small schools. In Modus many of the new schools occupy the same space as the school they replace, and most of the teachers are teachers from the former school. This is likely to compromise the autonomy of each of the new schools (Lee & Ready, 2007). There will be a tendency to respond to diseconomies of scale with shared AP courses and one band or football team. Some teachers will migrate between schools when this makes efficient use of resources. There will also be a temptation to preserve the departmental structure and the disciplinary allegiances of the old school. Math teachers will see other math teachers as their natural colleagues. There will be lines of consultation that will weaken loyalty to the new schools and preserve old ways of teaching.

In Operandi each school is a stand-alone school and the autonomy of each program is seen as important. Teachers in each school are encouraged to be colleagues with one another across areas of specialization. Loyalty to the school rather than to a subject area is encouraged. Successful schools are eventually organized into clusters and there is cooperation among different schools, but the emphasis is on learning from one another about how to have a successful school program rather than on cooperation among people with a common specialization. There is more sharing of ideas than pooling of resources. There is not a common band, common AP courses, or a common football team—at least not right away, at least not until identity of a strong community is well established.

What is wanted in scaling up is a process that starts new small schools as strong communities. What is to be avoided is a process that reduces the size of schools and hopes that something good will happen. Neither Modus nor Operandi is altogether guilty of the latter. Both begin their new schools with some conception of a shared educational project for the school and with a planning effort built around it. But Operandi does this better than Modus. This is the case because Operandi is better at respecting four important startup principles:

1. New small schools should be created as the result of a social contract between a group of founders and the school district. The social contract is granted on the basis of the acceptance of the schools' shared educational project. The school begins with committed leaders who share a coherent vision. Members of the school community are added to the school because they are committed to the shared educational project. Freedom of association is emphasized. Forced choice among limited options is minimized.
2. Adequate time for planning and professional development is essential. Creating good educational programs rooted in a coherent shared educational program is hard work. People need time to do it well. They may need the opportunity to consult with others or take courses to learn new ways of teaching.
3. The interactions between teachers that are important to developing professional community are structured so as to develop loyalty to

the school program as a whole. Loyalties built around discipline or areas of specialization should be secondary.

4. Successful small schools are used as resources to help new startups, and ideas are readily shared among small schools.

There is one more difference to take note of. While the new schools in Modus get their students from a school that is to be closed, in Operandi a wider range of students may choose the new school. In Operandi any student in the district may apply to any school. At the same time new small schools are thought to be especially important for those students who are currently served by underperforming schools. Thus new schools are located so as to make it easier for these students to attend. However, these weaker schools are not closed—at least not immediately.

The main point of this arrangement is to allow new schools to establish themselves as communities of the like-minded and to do so without the burden of a culture of failure. A second point is to encourage these schools to disproportionately serve those students currently served by poor schools. A third point is to provide an incentive to current schools to improve or run the risk of losing their students.

A potential downside of this arrangement is that new schools may cream from current ones. Those students most likely to migrate from poor schools to new small schools in their area may be the students (or their families) who are most engaged in their education and most motivated to seek good educational opportunities. But these students and their families may also be the ones who contribute most to the stability and success of their current schools. Operandi's way of creating small schools makes them rather like charter schools and gives them some features of magnet schools. Such schools in a system of mixed schools can make other schools worse by depriving them of their most engaged students and their families.

If so, and if district policy allows the number of small schools in the district to expand as demand and capacity permit, then it can be argued that this is largely a transition problem. If small schools are better schools for all students, then they should come to dominate their systems. Underperforming schools will improve or disappear. If there are students who will benefit from larger comprehensive schools, then these schools will continue with an appropriate student body.

Why not just quickly transform all schools in a district into small schools? There are two arguments against this. One is that while we can safely say that the idea that we should have small schools that are strong communities is a promising idea, we do not really know the potential of small schools. Nor do we know whom they will serve well or whom they will serve poorly. Second, any time we try to scale up a promising innovation, it is important to take the time to get it right. Haste is often a formula for failure.

Can our children wait? They can wait for us to try a promising yet largely untested innovation carefully. They can wait for us to think things through. They can wait for us to get it right. Education has a long and dishonorable list of half-baked and poorly thought out innovations rapidly implemented. We must not replicate these failures.

KEEPING ON: POLICIES FOR THRIVING SCHOOL COMMUNITIES

All schools need a policy environment that allows them to do their work successfully. Among the characteristics of a good policy environment is that it is stable and predictable. This is especially important for innovative school programs. They are not well served by a policy patchwork of easily revoked exemptions. If small schools that are strong communities are to thrive, districts and states must create a durable policy framework for them.

Part of creating a stable policy environment for small schools is a commitment to a set of policies for guiding the creation and the function of these small schools that is well articulated in advance. A second important ingredient is creating institutions that provide a voice and political clout for small schools at the district level. Small schools, like any innovative program, will have detractors and will offend vested interest. Contending with large school district politics is not a venture for the faint of heart. And it is difficult for innovative schools to function if their staff and their principal are constantly required to spend their time defending them or securing resources for them. If small schools are worth doing, they are worth doing right.

I cannot outline here anything like a complete set of policies and institutions for small schools. What I want to do is characterize what I think are essential policies for small schools that are strong communities. These policies might be thought of as a kind of social contract that districts have with their small schools. Some of what goes into such a social contract will be generic. That is, it will outline policies that govern all small schools. But some of what constitutes the social contract should be specific to each school. It will describe the shared educational project of the school and how the school will deal with a range of issues. The social contract should be in writing. It is, in effect, a charter for the school, although I prefer the term *social contract* both because it results in an agreement about how some aspect of our collective life will be regulated and because it avoids confusion with charter schools. Small schools may, but need not be, charter schools. In describing the idea of a social contract, I will consider five questions:

1. Why is a social contract important?
2. What is the essential content of the social contract between small schools, their school district, and their students and their families?
3. What kinds of autonomy do small schools require?
4. What systemic issues must we consider?
5. How do we provide for collaboration, professional development, and leadership development?

Why Have a Social Contract?

It is useful to think of a small school as rooted in a social contract that begins with the acceptance by a school board of a proposal for a school and becomes the basis for recruiting teachers and students. We can address many of the policy issues that need addressing by considering the district policies that set terms for this social contract.

There are a number of reasons why a new school should begin with a social contract. First, having such a contract helps to create a stable policy environment for small schools. Everyone knows what the rules and expectations are in advance. Second, seeing small schools as rooted in a social contract is a way of recognizing that they are both public schools and free associations. The public interest in small schools is protected through the process of approving a proposal and by the policy considerations that structure what is acceptable in a proposal. For example, small schools will have to say how they will promote equality of opportunity and create good citizens. At the same time, wide choice is provided to teachers, students, and their families to choose a school from among those the district has provided that satisfy their particular preferences.

Third, starting a school with a proposal that establishes a contract between the school and its district is a way of getting new schools started as strong communities. The proposal to the school board should describe the school's shared educational project and be evaluated on the basis of its coherence and feasibility. We do not start by downsizing and then asking those who wish to work in a new school to figure out what it is about.

Fourth, the existence of this social contract with the board can function as the basis of recruiting teachers and students. The coherence of the shared educational project can become the basis of the cohesion among the staff and students.

Finally, the social contract can be the basis of accountability. First and foremost, new small schools should be accountable for doing well what they promise to do. The social contract can describe what each school will be accountable for and how it will be evaluated.

The Contents of the Social Contract

Districts should lay out certain background conditions for the social contract. What I mean by background conditions are either conditions that all new schools must fulfill or questions that all new schools must address. District policies concerning background conditions should address at least these crucial questions: Are there curricular requirements? What are they? How are teachers to be hired and evaluated? How are students to be recruited? How are small schools to be held accountable? How are small schools to be funded?

What are the curricular requirements? While small schools that are strong communities should be able to have distinctive educational programs, there are also some core things they must teach. They must respect state law about the subjects to be taught. Since in urban districts student mobility is generally high, the curriculum must permit students to transfer. And students have a right to expect that they will receive an education that permits college entrance. Generally this means that small schools will need to teach a curriculum that includes algebra and a math sequence that builds on it, a foreign language, appropriate science courses, English, history, and social studies. Having an innovative program is a matter of how these subjects are taught, not whether they are taught.

There are also core purposes all schools must serve (Strike, 2008). We owe students an education that helps them to become autonomous. We owe them an education that provides adequate access to those social positions that are of economic and political import. And we owe them an education that gives them access to the diverse cultural riches of our society. Small schools can be evaluated not only as to whether they teach what must be taught, but whether they teach it in a way that accomplishes these goals.

How are teachers to be hired and evaluated? If we expect small schools to have a distinctive shared educational project and to achieve the coherence and cohesion that such a shared educational project enables, then they must be able to hire teachers who are philosophically compatible and decisions about their evaluation and retention should be made by the school. Moreover, I would prefer that those who teach in small schools be unionized. I do not wish the small schools movement to become an exercise in union busting. At the same time provisions must be made in at least three areas. Seniority provisions of the union contract cannot override the ability of small schools to make personnel judgments about their own teachers. Personnel policies, especially grievance procedures, cannot become a means to bureaucratize the relations between teachers, principals, and the district. Finally, community building should be a consideration in how teachers are paid. Whatever the virtues of merit pay, it is likely to be destructive of community. Moreover, teachers should be paid for a single job without additional compensation for such things as supervising extracurricular activities. This reflects a desire to have teachers committed to their school, its educational program, and its students rather than to teaching a subject where other activities are viewed as outside of the central role and thus require additional compensation.

How will students be recruited? Small schools that are strong communities need to be voluntary associations. Teachers need to choose to work in them because they are attuned to the shared educational project. Students need to attend because their families accept the schools' shared educational project. There are, however, a number of caveats about this.

While a student's family may choose a school, the school should not be able to choose among students. That a student's family wishes to enroll a student in a given small school community should be viewed as a sufficient reason to assume their acceptance of the school's shared educational project. If a school is oversubscribed, then choice among applicants should be made by lottery. The point of this policy is to prevent the kind of stratification of schools that might otherwise result from competitive admission or from screening interviews. School districts are responsible to provide information about their small schools that is adequate to enable a competent choice and school districts are responsible to ensure that parents who wish to enroll their children in a small school are familiar with this information and with their alternatives.

Districts must also make adequate provision for disabled students and students with limited English proficiency.

Finally, the school district is responsible for monitoring the racial and socioeconomic mix of its small schools and for acting to redress imbalances. It is now illegal (*Parents v. Seattle,* 2007) to employ race as an admissions criterion so as to achieve racial balance. Nevertheless, school districts can take the socioeconomic composition of their schools into account when designing admissions policy, and they can consider the effect of location and program on the composition of the student body. I do not believe that small schools should be asked to undertake a burden of integration that is not accepted by other schools in a district, but care should be taken that small schools do not increase racial or socioeconomic isolation.

How will we manage accountability? I view accountability as a crucial matter for small schools, and I will devote Chapter 9 to a discussion of it. Here I give a brief summary: The social contract with the school district needs to emphasize appropriate accountability. The core of the idea of appropriate accountability is that small schools should provide the education they promise to provide in their social contract, and they should provide it well. This means that a school's shared educational project should be the main basis of its accountability to the district. Small schools should explain how they will collect and present evidence that they are succeeding on their aspirations. It also means that accountability must be somewhat individualized at the school level. Different schools will have different shared educational projects. They should be accountable in ways that reflect these differences. Finally, it means that, insofar as districts are able, accountability should not be strongly tied to meeting benchmarks on any standardized test. I do think there is a role for standardized testing in education, but I do not believe that small schools should be at risk of sanction or closing because of such test scores. To make test scores central for small schools, especially small schools with a significant at-risk population, is essentially saying that their shared educational project is superseded by results on standardized tests. If we accept the shared educational project of a small school as describing a valued form of education, then this is what we need to hold the school responsible for providing.

How will we fund small schools? Districts need to spell out the resources that will be available for startup and for ongoing operations. These resource packages need to recognize that small schools may encounter certain diseconomies of scale. They may cost more, and they should not be put in the position of needing to raise funds for buildings and equipment. Districts might be advised to think of the costs of small schools in terms of costs per graduate rather than costs per pupil attending and to accept higher per-pupil costs. In the long run, if small schools are more successful, they will also be less expensive when all of the social costs are factored in. Students who drop out make less of a long-term contribution to our collective welfare and often generate substantial costs elsewhere.

Those who propose new small schools should be expected to provide a business plan that shows how their program can be operated on the basis of the resources they can expect to have.

Here is a set of questions that might serve as a model for an application, the acceptance of which will establish the social contract between a district and a new small school:

Model Application for Small Schools

1. Describe your shared educational project. Explain how you will create the elements that are essential to strong educational communities: coherence, cohesion, care, and connectivity. If your school has a theme or curricular focus, what is it? Why is it important?
2. Describe your curriculum and how you will meet basic legal requirements, provide for student transfer, and enable college entrance.

3. Describe how you will create a strong intellectual community with a commitment to treating subjects as practices and to authentic instruction and assessment.
4. Describe how you will create a strong democratic community. What are the common goods you will pursue? How will you show that you value your weakest members?
5. Describe the institutions and practices you will develop in order to create collegiality among teachers and shared democratic governance among the community's citizens.
6. Describe how you will hire and evaluate teachers.
7. Describe how you will recruit and admit students.
8. Describe how you will evaluate your programs and make improvements in the light of your evaluations.
9. Describe how you will be accountable to the district for doing well what you have proposed to do.
10. Provide a business plan that shows how you will operate a successful school with the resources with which you will be provided.

Autonomy

Much of what has been said above assumes that small schools that are strong communities need to be autonomous. Part of the point of establishing small schools through a social contract is to serve the public interest in education without significant bureaucratic control from the center. What kind of autonomy do small schools require?

They should be freestanding. That is, each small school must be an independent school with its own program, staff, principal, and students. Conversely, they should not be schools within schools or in any other way a piece of a larger and more integrated program. Freestanding schools have a number of advantages over schools within schools (Lee & Ready, 2007). Being a subset of a larger school easily creates a kind of between-school tracking system or status hierarchy. Loyalty to one's own school is weakened and reliance on departmental structures that cut across schools is encouraged. It becomes harder to have a distinct shared educational program when instructional resources are shared and students can migrate between schools for some purposes such as AP courses or sports. Thus, even when resource considerations require that more than one school inhabit a common facility, the freestanding character of each program should be insisted on.

Autonomy means substantial control over such things as the hiring and retention of teachers, program development, and resource allocation within the school so as to satisfy chosen priorities.

Autonomy means significant local governance and diminished external bureaucratic control.

If small schools are to be strong communities, they need to be autonomous in these and other ways. They need to be able to create a community of the like-minded.

Systemic Concerns About Small Schools

The creation of a number of small schools raises several systemic issues that concern equality. Two of these issues should be addressed: How will we avoid status hierarchies among different schools? How will we see to equal opportunity?

One of the dangers of small schools in large numbers is that status hierarchies can develop among them. This could be reputational. That is, for one reason or another some schools might get a reputation as good schools or easy schools or as schools for certain kinds of kids and not others. To some degree this is inevitable. At the same time it is worth monitoring and attending to, especially if these differences become expressed as differences in the racial or socioeconomic composition of the school. One reason for selecting students by lottery is to make it harder for initially successful schools to recruit academically more talented students or to exclude students who are not seen as desirable.

We should be especially careful not to build the potential for status hierarchies into the conception or even the names of new small schools. In their book on schools within schools Lee and Ready (2007) describe one school, Adams, that contains six subschools named Alternative, College Prep, Community, Core Curriculum, International/Cooperative Learning, and Vocational. These schools had significantly different status and some were more highly sought after than others. One result of this was that these schools generated significant differences in the racial and socioeconomic composition of the different schools. This, I believe, was predictable. When schools have names such as College Prep and Vocational, we have writ tracking large in the conception of our small schools. And it is undesirable because it is inconsistent with the democratic function of schooling.

I would, thus, not accept any mix of schools that included schools that reproduce a distinction between a college preparatory and a vocational track. I would not discourage schools with occupational themes, but these themes should not be of such a character that they are easily seen as nonacademic, and they should include a mix of occupations, many of which presuppose college attendance. For example, a school might emphasize biotechnology, and its graduates might go on to become professional biologists, zookeepers, florists, or dental technicians. Here the occupational theme is not likely to produce socioeconomic stratification between schools. Moreover, I would expect all schools to have an academic core of those subjects that can lead to college admission. These courses need not be organized in the traditional way–indeed, they need not be organized as distinct subject areas. They might be woven into a particular theme.

Inequality of opportunity can be a result of differential treatment within schools, but it may also result from differences between schools. Which students are small schools for? One response is that they are disproportionately for at-risk students or for students whose current schools are failing. Is this what we want?

There is a case for saying "Yes." I have argued that small schools that are strong communities are a cure for alienation. Perhaps they are most appropriate for those most likely to be alienated. Another possibility is suggested by a recent study of New York City charter schools that makes two notable claims: The first is that charter schools produce higher levels of achievement than do other public schools for comparable kids. The second is that charter schools are disproportionately attended by poor black children (Hoxby & Murarka, 2007). If both claims are true, then charter schools in New York promote equality of opportunity because they improve the performance of schools attended by the most at-risk students. Perhaps small schools should be largely for poor and minority kids.

I am distrustful of this line of argument. We have known since the publication of James Coleman's (1968) work on inequality of opportunity that poverty affects educational results and that concentrating poor children in schools has negative consequences for their achievement. We should avoid conceptualizing the role of small schools or locating them in such a way as to increase racial or socioeconomic isolation.

A second difficulty is that we need to be concerned not only for the welfare of students who attend small schools, but also for the welfare of the students who remain in the schools from which these students are drawn. We can reduce the potential for small schools to cream the best students from other schools by admitting students through a lottery. Nevertheless, the very fact that a student applies to attend a school of choice suggests that this student's family is invested in his or her education. Such investment makes the student's family an asset for a school. If small schools draw desirable students or motivated families from weak schools, that may make the feeder schools worse.

Nor is there any reason to suppose that small schools are uniquely appropriate for poor or minority populations. Students of all races and classes can be alienated. We might have learned this from the tragedy at Columbine High (Raywid & Osiyama, 2000). Students of all races and classes need to be taught in an environment that is nurturing and need to learn to see subjects as practices. There is nothing in the conception of communities of practice or democratic communities that makes them especially appropriate for students of a particular race or class. Thus I would prefer that we think of small schools as similar to magnet schools in that they are open to all students in the district and are attractive enough that students from all walks of life will want to attend. We need policies that help small schools to be more rather than less inclusive of racial and socioeconomic diversity. Thinking of them as for at-risk students seems not a progressive view.

Leadership and Professional Development

If small schools that are strong communities are different, if they provide a kind of education not often provided in other schools, then teachers will need to learn from other teachers how to function in them and leaders for such schools will have to be developed. One way to do this is to organize small schools into clusters. Clusters can provide means of collaboration and sharing of ideas about good practice. New teachers or teachers in new schools can learn from experienced hands. Clusters can be places that identify and prepare the next generation of leaders for small schools.

While one can hope that in the future there will be teacher training programs and leadership training programs that prepare professionals to work in such schools, there are now few such programs. What is needed is institutions that provide for collegiality and for apprenticeships across small schools. The creation of clusters that perform these tasks should be considered an important part of developing institutions to sustain small schools that are strong communities.

SUMMARY

I have described small schools that are strong communities as rooted in a kind of social contract between each school and its district. This, in turn, has been part of a characterization of a policy environment that will produce good starts and strong continuance. The crucial point is to create strong voluntary educational communities with a shared educational project that is there from the beginning, rather than simply to create small schools and hope that something good will happen. A good small school is more than just a school with fewer students. It is a place where teaching is different, school culture is different, and governance is different. These kinds of schools can happen systematically only if districts commit themselves to policies that allow small schools to be created and operated by those with a shared vision for a distinctive form of good education. Emphasizing a policy environment in which small schools are rooted in a social contract first with their school boards and then with their students and their families is a way of providing the autonomy needed while protecting the public interest in education.

CHAPTER 8

Community and Small Schools

A New Paradigm for School Reform

Educational policy analysts, funders, educational leaders, and policymakers agree that the value of education can largely be framed in terms of human capital development and can be measured by assessments of standardized test results and graduation rates. . . . In addition, these stakeholders generally profess a concern for the degree to which such outcomes are equal across different demographic categories and for the degree to which different groups of students are receiving equal opportunities to achieve such outcomes. There is also a concern for efficiency–that is, value is placed on less costly ways to achieve desired results and on effective implementation of educational opportunities.

–Joseph Kahne, *Values and Evidence*

In the attempt to create small schools that are strong communities, we have something more than a useful add-on to current pictures of school reform, something more than a new educational technique, something more than a better way to help kids improve test scores. We have a view that challenges the policy outlook that Kahne describes in the quote above. We have a distinct paradigm of school reform and a distinct vision of the nature of a good education, which differs from other views in its goals and educational strategies. It also differs in its understanding of the core problems school reform needs to solve and how to solve them and in what it sees as evidence of success. Alienation is the problem; community is the cure. We will know we have succeeded when we have evidence of authentic learning as a consequence of authentic teaching. We will know we have succeeded when our schools produce autonomous individuals, citizens who care for the common good, and people who find that their education has enriched their lives.

In this chapter I develop this idea that an emphasis on community allied with small schools is the basis of a new paradigm for school reform, and I distinguish the assumptions on which this paradigm rests from those that underlie standards-based reform and choice. Why is this important? It is important, first because we need a genuine alternative to current models of school reform—an alternative that does not just try to tinker current efforts into success. The kinds of reforms that we have pursued since *A Nation at Risk* have given us very little, and it is becoming clear that the aspirations of No Child Left Behind are unrealistic (Rothstein, 2002, 2004). Moreover, the pressures that its accountability measures put on educators produce numerous undesirable side effects (Nichols & Berliner, 2007a; Rothstein et al., 2008). We need to consider the possibility that the assumptions that underlie modern efforts are flawed and look for better assumptions to guide our efforts.

Second, if reform efforts rooted in the assumption that schools should be communities are to be successful, clarity is needed about core assumptions. Even hopeful school reforms can fail if they lack a coherent vision of their project. If they lack such clarity, they will undergo death by a thousand compromises, accommodations, and misunderstandings. And they will be perceived as just another way to succeed in raising test scores. Chapter 6 suggested that we may already see this happening to the small schools movement as it struggles to scale up. It seems in danger of being reduced to the idea that if we can just make schools small, something good will happen. The idea that small schools need to be strong communities has not adequately caught hold. Effective reform requires clarity about fundamental assumptions.

THE IDEA OF A PARADIGM

The concept of a paradigm—in simple terms, a theoretical framework—was popularized in academic circles by Thomas Kuhn (1970) in *The Structure of Scientific Revolutions*. In this book Kuhn argued that we can divide scientific research into two phases. The first he called "normal science"; the second, "revolutionary science." The processes of normal science involve the application and elaboration of a paradigm to scientific research. Revolutionary science occurs when a paradigm fails and is replaced by another. Revolutionary science results in a *paradigm shift:* a new way of thinking.

The essence of the idea of a paradigm is that scientific research programs (and, I believe, systematic thought about pretty much everything) are rooted in some fundamental ideas about how the world works or ought to work (Strike, 1979). These core ideas structure inquiry. They indicate what the relevant problems to be solved are, what counts as a plausible solution to these problems, and what counts as relevant evidence that the problems have been solved.

Some of Kuhn's historical work focused on the transition from a geocentric picture of the universe to a heliocentric one. The *geocentric* picture of the universe assumes that the earth is the fixed center of the universe and that the sun, moon, stars, and planets revolve around the earth in perfect circles. Unfortunately this picture has serious difficulties. The planets do not seem to orbit the earth as one would expect on the assumptions of the geocentric theory. In fact, they appear to march across the sky against the background of the "fixed" stars only to reverse their course for a while before continuing on their journey. We know today that this retrograde motion is an illusion explained by the movement of the earth around the sun, but this is an account that could not be held by geocentric astronomers since they assumed that the earth was the fixed center of the universe. Geocentric astronomers solved the problem by introducing what they called *epicycles*–smaller circles inside of the larger circles that describe the orbits of the planets around the earth. The planets, it seems, take little circular detours. That is OK: Circles are the perfect form of motion and the heavens were created perfect.

Epicycles helped to reconcile theory with observation, but not in an especially satisfying way. There was no good reason for epicycles except for the fact that observations required them. As the data about planetary motion got better, more epicycles were required. Eventually the research program was an ad hoc mess; in Kuhn's charming phrase, it was "awash in a sea of anomalies." A new paradigm was needed. This was provided by Copernicus who put the sun at the center of the solar system–the *heliocentric theory*. It was improved by Kepler who substituted ellipses for circles and described planetary orbits mathematically and by Newton whose laws of gravitation accounted for these orbits and a good deal more.

An important point about paradigms is that they are not easily refuted by negative empirical evidence or, in the case of policy, by failure. Moreover, new paradigms often involve new views about what the relevant problems to be solved are and what counts as evidence that they have been solved. As a consequence, they will often seem absurd to those working in the old paradigm. It will seem far more reasonable to continue to try to fix the old paradigm–to continue to do basically what has always been done. Geocentric astronomers did not just observe retrograde motion, throw up their hands, and immediately abandon their core ideas. They experimented with various ideas about how their observations could be reconciled with their theories. They engaged in the kind of problem solving that Kuhn calls normal science. And this is perfectly proper. Paradigms are not refuted by a few negative observations; they are eroded by the persistent failure to get the paradigm to work over time. New paradigms, in turn, are disorienting and seem unreasonable at their inception. This is the attitude we should take toward school reform paradigms. It is not one failure that refutes them. It is a history of failure and a constant need to discover new strategies to salvage old ideas.

When does a history of failure mean we should look elsewhere for better assumptions? There is no formula to address this question. It is a matter of judgment, and reasonable people can disagree. Should we not view current views of school reform as failed paradigms? It is my judgment that we should. Despite various waves of reform since *A Nation at Risk*, the quality of American education has not greatly improved. We could, of course, treat every modest success as evidence that the current reform is working and every failure as evidence of the need for more persistence and better implementation. But perhaps we should begin to critique the assumptions on which these old paradigms rest and ask if it is not time for a bit of revolutionary thinking about how to proceed with school reform.

TWO PARADIGMS FOR REFORM: STANDARDS AND CHOICE

The two existing paradigmatic views I will contrast with the "community paradigm" are standards-based reform–the "standards paradigm"–and market-oriented choice–the "choice paradigm." The first emphasizes the use of standards and accountability to reform education. The second emphasizes the creation of a free market for education. I begin my examination of each paradigm by asking two central questions: What does this view see as the crucial problem to be solved by school reform? What is the basic character of a solution? After addressing these questions I then expand the description of each view into other areas of concern.

The Standards Paradigm

The standards paradigm has been the major attempt to reform schools by improving their management by government. It has had two major recent incarnations. The first was best captured by Goals 2000 (1994), the signature school reform initiative of the Clinton administration. The second is captured by No Child Left Behind (2002), the Bush administration's contribution to education reform.

Advocates of the earlier phase of standards-based reform had two overriding objectives (Fuhrman, 1993; Strike, 1997). The first was excellence. The American educational system was viewed as too soft, too unconcerned with academic achievement. Something needed to be done to instill a sense of rigor in the system. The second goal was coherence. The system was viewed as failing because it was incoherent. Its various parts–curriculum, teacher training, funding, testing, and professional development–were not "aligned" with one another. Thus they were not mutually reinforcing.

Suppose we–the state–want to do a couple of seemingly simple things. We want to train teachers to effectively teach the curriculum they will encounter in the schools in which they will work, and we want to test students to see if they have mastered this curriculum. The results on these tests can provide research to improve schools and direct resources where they are needed. Unfortunately, without statewide standards we can do neither of these things because the curriculum varies from school to school. What gets taught in any given school is the result of complex interactions among textbook publishers, teachers associations, state governments, local school boards, school administrations, and individual teachers. At a statewide level we simply do not know in a detailed way what is being taught in most schools. If we do not know this, we cannot train teachers properly or test students to see what they have learned. The various parts of the educational system are not aligned and therefore are not mutually reinforcing.

The solution to both the problem of excellence and the problem of coherence was standards that would be created at the state or national level. These standards would be rigorous, world-class. Moreover, they would be the key to the coherence of the educational system. Once a state had standards that defined what it wanted children to know and be able to do, it would be able to align teacher education, testing, professional development, resource allocation, and accountability so as to make the entire system more efficient and effective.

In recent years the emphasis concerning the role of standards has shifted away from the emphasis on creating a coherent system and toward a more exclusive emphasis on accountability. Of course, accountability has always been a part of the package. Under the influence of Goals 2000 many states created high school exit tests that students had to pass if they were to graduate. But as the aspirations of systemic reform faded, accountability increasingly became the centerpiece of standards-based reform. Certainly it is at the center of No Child Left Behind.

No Child Left Behind created an escalating set of test-defined benchmarks that schools must meet. All schools must test (almost) all children in mathematics and reading in every grade from the third grade to the eighth grade. Moreover they must disaggregate scores for different populations and report test scores for each group. Each year the percentage of children who must score "proficient" or above on these tests increases. If schools fail to meet their annual yearly progress goals, there are a set of sanctions they must undergo.

Given this, we can add another claim about what standards-based reform sees as the central problem to be solved. It is the lack of accountability. Educators are not held accountable for producing results. The solution is an elaborate set of test-defined benchmarks, incentives, and penalties.

The Choice Paradigm

There are numerous variations on the choice paradigm (Brighouse, 2000). Some choice advocates have advocated statewide voucher systems. No state has as yet adopted such a plan. Charter schools are another variation. While charter schools are publicly funded, they are operated by groups other than the local educational authority. This may be a group of citizens, a group of teachers, or a private corporation. Charter schools generally have significant relief from the regulations that govern other public schools in their areas. The students who attend charter schools must choose them. Funding follows students. If a charter school does not attract enough students it will fail. A majority of states have made provision for charter schools.

A third variation on choice is to provide vouchers or the opportunity to transfer to poor students or to students whose schools are failing. Milwaukee and Cleveland have needs-tested voucher plans. No Child Left Behind has provisions that make vouchers available to children in persistently failing schools.

By far the dominant motive among policy makers for advocating choice is the belief that competition is crucial to the reform of schools. If schools must compete for their students, they will be better schools. We should, however, be clear that there are other motives. Some choice advocates (Brighouse, 2000) see choice of the right kind as a significant factor in the pursuit of equal opportunity. Some are motivated by the desire to secure public funding for religious education. Some choice advocates (I among them) see choice as a requirement of creating schools that are communities. In describing the choice paradigm, I will emphasize the views of those who desire choice because they see competition as crucial to educational reform because this is the vision of choice that has tended to frame the policy argument about school reform.

For choice advocates there are two core problems that choice can solve. One is the lack of freedom that results from a publicly managed school system. The second is the inherent inefficiency of public bureaucracies including public schools. The solution is to allow the market to work its magic by using choice to create competition. Education is to be improved by Adam Smith's (1776/2000) invisible hand.

An important commitment for those who advocate choice and whose views reflect free market ideals is consumer sovereignty. Consumer sovereignty has two elements. The first is that in a free society people are entitled to want what they want and to use their resources to satisfy their preference in the market. Consumer preferences and consumer choices have a kind of normative force (Monk, 1990). What is produced, sold, and purchased should be a function of what people want and can afford, not of government decision making.

The second element is that in a free society self-interested producers can be expected to respond to the preferences that individuals bring to the market by trying to satisfy these preferences. And they will compete with other providers to attract consumers. In a free society, consumers vote with their purchases. That is how power (accountability) is rightfully exercised over the decisions of producers—one dollar, one vote. Unencumbered free choices make market economies efficient because producers must satisfy consumers.

There are limits to consumer sovereignty that market advocates often recognize. Consumer sovereignty provides access to goods and services proportionately to the ability to pay. If we apply this to education, it would seem that an unqualified commitment to consumer sovereignty would lead to the denial of education to the children of those who are unable to pay for it, and those with more assets would get more and better education than those with fewer assets. This is inconsistent with equality of opportunity, a point that most choice advocates grant in some measure.

Market advocates also hold that markets are not always responsive to preferences. Suppose that you produce some good, *G*, that I wish to purchase. However, if I purchase *G*, it turns out that some of the benefits of my purchase of *G* inevitably go to other people who have not paid for them. Under such conditions markets will not work. For example, suppose you have produced a technology to provide clean air. I desire clean air. But I cannot pay you to produce it for me without enabling others to enjoy clean air as well. Moreover, there is no way to get these others to share the costs of clean air with me, and I am unable or unwilling to pay the full costs for benefits that these others enjoy. You are unable or unwilling to produce clean air for what I am willing or able to pay. The result is that market transactions will not provide clear air. Producers cannot recoup a fair price for what they produce because consumers are unable or unwilling to pay for benefits that go to others and there is no way to get these others to pay. Goods of this sort are said to involve neighborhood effects or externalities and are called public goods (not common goods).

One of the solutions to this dilemma is to have those goods where there are significant externalities provided by the government and paid for by taxes. Among the goods that are thought to be public goods (at least in part) are sewers, the military, and education. Milton Freidman (1962), whose work has had a profound effect on the views of choice advocates, says the following about education as a public good:

> A stable and democratic society is impossible without a minimum degree of literacy and knowledge on the part of most citizens and without widespread acceptance of some common set of values. Education can contribute to both. In consequence the gain from the education of a child accrues not only to the child or to his parents but also to other members of the society. The education of my child contributes to your welfare by promoting a stable and democratic society. It is not feasible to identify the particular individuals (or families) benefited and so to charge for the services rendered. There is therefore a significant "neighborhood effect." (p. 86)

The conclusion that Freidman draws is that education is appropriately mandated and paid for by government. However, Freidman also claims that the fact that education is a public good is not a reason why schools should be operated by government. In fact, there are advantages to having governments fund, but not operate, schools. One is freedom. If governments were to fund, but not operate, schools, people would be able to provide an education for their children that more adequately reflected their own preferences. A second reason is that government operation of schools creates a monopoly. Monopolies eliminate competition and are thus inefficient providers. An educational system in which schools had to compete for their students would be more efficient.

A Comparison of Paradigms

I can now summarize the core assumptions of the two existing paradigms considered above along with the new community paradigm for the purpose of comparing and contrasting their respective assumptions.

Paradigmatic Assumptions

The Community Paradigm–schools as communities
> *Core problem:* alienation, disengaged students
> *Key solution:* strong community fostered by small schools with an emphasis on authentic education, the mastery of practices, and democratic community

The Standards Paradigm–standards-based reform
> *Core problems:* lack of rigor, systemic coherence, and accountability
> *Key solutions:* standards, an aligned educational system, and accountability

The Choice Paradigm–market-oriented choice
> *Core problems:* lack of consumer choice and inefficiency of public monopolies.
> *Key solutions:* choice, markets, and competition

MOTIVATION AND MORE

Of course there is more to these paradigms than the core assumptions presented in the preceding section. These core commitments are connected to assumptions about human motivation, governance, teaching and learning, accountability, the purposes of education, and equality of opportunity. In this section I am going to sketch out how these paradigms play out with respect to these matters.

Motivation

How do these paradigms see motivation? The standards paradigm and the choice paradigm both emphasize external motivation in the form of incentives and sanctions. In the case of the standards paradigm, incentives are created by government. In the case of the choice paradigm, they are created by the market. While the emphasis in both cases is on incentives for educators, reformers have also viewed high-stakes tests as incentives for students (Bishop, 1989; Shanker, 1994). Both the standards paradigm and the choice paradigm accept Smith's (1776/2000) assumption that people are largely motivated by their own welfare, but the standards paradigm rejects the invisible hand.

The community paradigm emphasizes the social character of motivation and the capacity for people to be motivated by common goods. While community advocates need not disavow the use of external motivators, intrinsic motivation is emphasized and preferred. The emphasis is on the process of normation. Authentic instruction is used to help students see the point of the practices they are engaged in and internalize the value of the goods to which these practices lead. For teachers, intrinsic motivation flows from the value they attach to the good of the practices they teach, their internalized commitment to professional standards, their commitment to the community and its students, and trust. These forms of motivation are reinforced by collegiality with like-minded individuals.

The standards paradigm and the choice paradigm tend to miss the extent to which motives are socialized and often act as though they were simply innate or fixed. They also assume that people are largely self-interested in their motives. What this means in practice is that students and educators are viewed as motivated largely by such goods as income, status, and success. Both paradigms tend to assume possessive individualism in their assumptions about the springs of action.

It is, however, central to a theory of community that motivation is highly social and can involve shared goals. People tend to internalize the values of the communities to which they belong; moreover, internalizing these values helps reinforce community and enhances belonging. Children internalize the values of their caregivers, and students internalize the values of their teachers when these teachers are seen as valuing them. Students come to care about the goods internal to practices when teachers who value them also value these goods and when these commitments are consistently reinforced by a good educational community. Finally, trust is both a condition of community and is enhanced when others in a community are seen as working toward shared goals.

Educational Goals

For the standards paradigm, standards are sometimes seen as chosen democratically by the legislature or its agents (O'Day & Smith, 1993) although the actual process has generally involved committees of teachers and subject matter experts, sometimes with a public hearing process as well. There is little in the theory of standards that requires any particular core aims. Nevertheless, as the quote from Kahne at the beginning of this chapter indicates, the prevailing assumption among advocates of the standards paradigm is that the core goals of education are human capital formation and the individual success and collective productivity that allegedly follow. Schooling is expected to prepare students for either higher education or work. Its role is to allow students to pursue self-chosen goals by making them economically competent–a process that also enhances collective productivity.

The standards paradigm tends to see goals such as productivity and competitiveness as public goods rather than common goods. That is, enhanced productivity and competitiveness are not seen as common goods to be collectively achieved through cooperative action. They are rather goods that the market does not provide or provide adequately and that must therefore be provided through government action.

In theory, the choice paradigm does not have a preferred set of goals. While it acknowledges that schools are publicly funded because they serve public goods, Friedman (1962) suggests that these place little constraint on what schools do. Moreover, the notion of consumer sovereignty suggests that schools should serve the preferences of consumers as expressed through the choices of consumers. It is not the role of government to shape these preferences. If consumer sovereignty rules, then the view of educational goals that choice advocates should recommend is "Let a thousand flowers bloom."

In fact, however, most choice advocates do not adopt a "let a thousand flowers bloom" philosophy. The rhetoric of choice advocates, so far as goals are concerned, does not seem to differ significantly from that of those who promote standards. Individual success in the market and productivity are viewed as the goals of education. And choice advocates often want standards too, although they are inclined to see them as means to provide consumer information.

The community paradigm has a broader vision of core educational goals. While, to be sure, human capital is important, schools are seen as concerned with enriching life. The goods internal to practices are valued. Education is seen as humane and humanistic. Citizenship, civic participation, and quality relationships are valued. Autonomy is important. The goods pursued are common goods as well as public goods. Pursuing these goods together in a community of shared purpose is itself valued.

What we should notice here is that for both the standards paradigm and the choice paradigm there is something of a discursive deficit so far as meaningful discussion of educational goals is concerned. These views are not essentially views about what education is for. They are views about organizational efficiency. They pose government management against the market–Max Weber's bureaucracy (see Camic, 2005) versus Adam Smith's (1776/2000) invisible hand. The standards paradigm's preference for a standardized curriculum offered to all children is not rooted in a conviction that certain goals are essential and that a standardized curriculum serves them. It is rooted in the requirements of creating an educational system and of accountability.

For the choice paradigm there is a theoretical preference for diverse goals. The idea of consumer sovereignty seems to require this. However, choice advocates rarely actually argue this. They, like standards advocates, take human capital development as the goal of education uncritically and without serious discussion. Thus human capital formation tends to be the default for both paradigms. Given this, it is perhaps a matter of interest that there is a great deal of evidence that Americans value a wider range of educational goals than human capital formation, productivity, and individual economic success. Rothstein et al. (2008), for example, claims that both polling data and various historical reports about the purposes of American education suggest eight goals for American education, including citizenship, appreciation of the arts and music, critical thinking, and emotional health. Yet despite their widespread public support these kinds of goals often get only lip service from both the standards and the choice paradigms and are often the kinds of goals that are easily pushed aside by narrow visions of accountability. Both the standards paradigm and the choice paradigm seem to see schools as the servants of a commercial republic rather than the servants of a democratic polity.

Curriculum and Pedagogy

The idea that schools should be communities emphasizes the idea that genuine learning is the initiation into communities of practice, and it values authentic teaching and learning. It has a set of core goals and believes that certain academic subjects tend to promote these core goals. At the same time, depth is preferred over coverage. Moreover, while there is a commitment to teaching academic subjects, it is not assumed that they must be taught in conventional ways. Schools may have a theme, and history, for example, can be woven into the theme–or the theme into history. The idea that schools should be communities emphasizes a common curriculum at the building level. While students in different schools may have quite different experiences, the emphasis on community favors a shared experience for students in a given school.

Standards advocates have not been of one mind about the curriculum or about the nature of good teaching. There has been a tendency to prefer a curriculum dominated by academic subjects. This has been viewed as more rigorous and therefore better. But, just as there has been surprisingly little debate about what education is for, there has also been surprisingly little debate about why a largely academic curriculum is the one most likely to promote human capital development. Yet when standards and accountability are applied at the high school level, the tendency has been to promote a common core of academic subjects. New York State, for example, requires that all students pass tests in five subjects–English, history, global studies, science, and math–in order to graduate.

For choice advocates, there is no preferred theory of the curriculum or of teaching. Here, too, the preferences of consumers should largely determine the curriculum and how it is taught. Educational practices will ultimately be determined by the choices consumers make. At the same time (and inconsistently), choice advocates sometimes follow the lead of standards advocates urging an academic curriculum for all.

Governance and Organizational Structure

For the community paradigm, schools should be locally and democratically governed. There should be a collegium where teachers have a dominant voice in those areas where training and experience are important. And there should be mechanisms that encourage widespread voice and participation of the entire school community in its affairs. Local governance requires significant autonomy at the building level. The organization is flat, democratic, and nonbureaucratic. Norms are complied with because they are shared and seen as the norms of the community rather than because compliance is enforced. The organization encourages personalization and a sense of membership.

For the choice paradigm, schools are operated by service providers–those who wish to operate a school and compete in the market. Such schools require significant autonomy even if they are quasi public, as are charter schools. They are, in this way, similar to schools that are communities. However, governance by provider is different in a significant way. The schools as communities paradigm seeks governance that is by the community. But on the choice model providers may be of different types including for-profit corporations. While under the choice paradigm schools may be democratically governed, the primary way in which consumers of education exercise power is through their choices.

The standards paradigm tends to centralize and bureaucratize governance. It alters the relationships among local schools, school districts, and state governments in a way that makes the authority of the state legislature more important. Standards are typically created at the state level. Hence the standards paradigm especially centralizes authority over goals and the curriculum. Moreover, when accountability becomes central and is linked to various rewards and sanctions, it tends to locate additional authority in state governments and in the national government. It tends to substitute compliance for reflection and takes decision making out of the hands of the community and those who do the work.

Core Moral Norms

The choice paradigm and the standards paradigm both tend to view equality of opportunity as their central norm. They do this because they tend to see their tasks in largely individualistic terms. Their role is to prepare students to participate in a society that distributes its goods and services through the operation of markets. Hence students in schools are seen as in competition for positions in higher education and for jobs, income, and status. Equality of educational opportunity aims to ensure that this competition is fair.

The community paradigm accepts that such competition is a part of the reality of our society. Hence it values equality of educational opportunity. However, it also sees part of its role as the creation of a democratic community in which all are valued equally apart from their role as producers and consumers. Hence it also values democratic inclusion and the collective pursuit of common goods.

Accountability

Accountability has become central to school reform. It is sufficiently important that I will devote the next chapter to its discussion. Here a brief summary of how the paradigms differ will suffice. Most views of accountability make assumptions about to whom educators are accountable and for what. On the standards paradigm, educators are generally viewed as accountable for meeting test-defined benchmarks. Typically they are accountable to a state legislature or its agents. Under No Child Left Behind they are accountable to Congress and its agents.

In theory, the choice paradigm makes educators accountable to consumers for satisfying their preferences. They may also be accountable to various legislatures for securing the public goods that are associated with schooling (Friedman, 1962). In fact the story is more complex since some choice advocates also support standards based accountability.

The community paradigm emphasizes accountability to the community for self-chosen goals as well as for meeting professional standards. Here too educators are also responsible for securing public goods.

It is important to note here how the story about accountability and governance mesh–not surprising since accountability is a part of governance and attempts to make educators accountable shape governance. Standards-based accountability is not the only thing that has centralized governance and taken decision making away from local schools and local districts, but it is the main thing.

A THIRD WAY OF SCHOOL REFORM

In this chapter I have discussed in depth the assumptions of the two existing paradigms of school reform–standards and choice–amd compared them to each other and to the assumptions of the idea of community allied with small schools in order to show that there is a new, third paradigm of school reform–the community paradigm. Table 8.1 provides a useful summary of the assumptions I've discussed.

The assumptions of each paradigm hang together. What connects the assumptions of the standards paradigm and the choice paradigm are a kind of individualism, the notion that education is concerned with public goods, not common goods, and the assumption that the essential aims of education are the economic competence of individuals and the collective productivity of society. This generates a view of schooling that seeks to serve the private aims of individual students while also satisfying the public good of productivity. Motivation for students and for teachers is extrinsic–success, money, security. In both the standards and the choice paradigms, schools are dominated by competition for those educational goods that have market value. Their core moral norm is equality of educational opportunity, which is essentially a norm of fair competition. Their ethos is that of possessive individualism: get an education to get a good job to get stuff. They are more like banks or shopping malls than they are like guilds, orchestras or congregations. YOYO ("You're on your own"), not WITT ("We're in this together") dominates.

The choice paradigm and the standards paradigm differ largely over whether efficient education is best provided by a state bureaucracy that sets standards, makes policies, monitors compliances, and enforces sanctions, or whether efficient education is best provided through the market. This debate has dominated thought about educational policy for several decades, and it was the core debate underlying No Child Left Behind, which is an incoherent compromise between the two views. The mix of standards and penalties says, in effect, that we will try standards-based accountability, and where that fails, we will try choice.

That the argument between choice and standards is an important one should not, however, cause us to overlook the ways in which these two views

TABLE 8.1. Three Paradigms for School Reform

	Community Paradigm	Standards Paradigm	Choice Paradigm
Core Problems	Alienation	Lack of a coherent system Lack of rigor Lack of accountability	Lack of freedom Inefficiency of monopolies
Key Solutions	Community	Standards Alignment Accountability	Choice Competition
Motivation	Intrinsic Professional standards Commitment to community Care Trust	Extrinsic Accountability-based incentives Merit pay	Extrinsic Market-based incentives
Educational Goals	Goods internal to practices Autonomy Citizenship Ethical relationships Individual success Collective productivity Common goods	State-defined standards Core aim is economic Individual success Collective productivity Public goods	Offered by producer Chosen by consumer Individual success Collective productivity Public goods
Curriculum and Pedagogy	Initiation into practices Authentic instruction Depth over coverage Core humanistic curriculum Themed or otherwise focused Shared curriculum	Curriculum defined by standards Real curriculum specified by tests	Offered by producer Chosen by consumer
Governance	Local at building level High autonomy A collegium of teachers Community participation Small, flat, nonbureaucratic	Legislative democracy Bureaucratic Monitoring for compliance Enforced sanctions	Consumer sovereignty Governance by provider Autonomy
Core Norms	Equal opportunity Democratic inclusion	Equal opportunity	Equal opportunity
Accountability	To: Local community For: Professional standards, meeting local goals, care for community To: Legislature For: Public interest	To: Legislature For: Test-defined benchmarks	To: Consumer For: Satisfaction of preferences To: Legislature For: Public interest

are similar, the assumptions they share, and the degree to which these assumptions are profoundly anticommunal.

The community paradigm is radically different. While it does not dispute the fact that where wants outstrip resources there will be competition, it emphasizes common goods, shared goals, and democratic inclusion.

One of the ways in which the community paradigm differs from standards and choice is that it is rooted in what might be called (following Martha Nussbaum, 1990) a thick but vague conception of human flourishing. This conception is not neutral about the human good. While it is big-tented, believing that its vision of human flourishing is consistent with most religions and cultures, it nevertheless claims that autonomy and a life where the goods internal to practices are a significant source of human happiness are central human goods, as are democratic citizenship and meaningful and ethical human relationships. When these educational goals are rejected, as they are by some modern fundamentalisms and by the philistinism of possessive individualism, the community paradigm seeks to defend them. And it insists that these goods and goals are best pursued in community.

Thus the community paradigm is profoundly different from the standards and choice paradigms. We should not see it as just another technique to be employed in trying to succeed on standards-based reform. It is not just a response to the failure of other paradigms. It involves a different and a better vision of human flourishing. It is a third way.

CHAPTER 9

Community and Accountability

Tests are not very effective at evaluating, and hence promoting, twenty-first century skills such as problem solving, team work, and collaboration within diverse environments. Ultimately employers are not looking for students who can fill in bubble sheets on tests. Instead they are looking for students who can function effectively in a global and fast-changing world.
–Ladd, *Holding Schools Accountable Revisited*

Schools with the largest gains in student achievement place much more emphasis on academic excellence as opposed to "the basics," occupational skills, or good work habits. Their goals are also clearer: their staffs are more likely to agree on priorities such as the mastery of subject matter and the development of student self-esteem and efficacy. In a word, they are more likely to perceive the school as having a mission.
–Chubb, "Why the Current Wave of School Reform Will Fail"

In Ithaca, New York, a new charter school, New Roots Charter School, is to be opened in the fall of 2009. Their Web site (http://www.newrootsschool.org) describes their mission as follows:

> New Roots Charter School empowers young people to learn actively, think critically, solve problems creatively and collaboratively, and develop the knowledge and skills to redesign our communities for social, economic, and ecological sustainability.

New Roots (as its founders conceive it) seems to exemplify quite well the features that I argued characterized schools that are communities. It is small, themed, and focused. It has a sense of mission. It seeks to attract faculty and students who are committed to the mission. It is part of a consortium of schools with similar missions (http://greencharterschools.org/).

How should New Roots and schools like it be held accountable? Like almost all high schools in New York, New Roots must give New York State Regents Exams to all its students. They must pass these tests to graduate.

Like all public schools in the United States, it must test its students in reading and math once while they are in high school. Is student performance on such tests an adequate basis for holding the school accountable? These tests do not seem to hold New Roots accountable for succeeding on its distinctive purposes.

Suppose that New Roots's students did less well on state tests than those students who attend Ithaca High School, would we consider the school to have been a failure? Suppose that graduates were less likely to attend prestigious universities than Ithaca High graduates, but were more likely to seek occupations that emphasized "redesign[ing] our communities for social, economic, and ecological sustainability," would we consider the school to be a success–even if students did less well on more conventional measures? How will New Roots be held accountable for succeeding on its own mission? Does the fact that it is accountable to New York State for getting its kids past the Regent Exams make it harder to succeed on its mission?

Schools that are communities need a view of accountability that locates accountability largely in the local school community and that holds schools accountable for succeeding on the full range of goals they aim to achieve. They need a view of accountability that encourages authentic teaching and learning, and they need a view of accountability that helps educators to take responsibility for their own work. They need a view of accountability that encourages curricular focus and local vision. They need a view of accountability that encourages the growth of the school program and the people that offer it. Ultimately, they need a vision of accountability that encourages good and strong educational communities.

Current views of accountability that emphasize meeting test-defined benchmarks accomplish none of these things very well. Instead, they take authority away from those who do the work, discourage authentic teaching, enforce curricular uniformity, undermine commitment and intrinsic motivation, and create an alienated work force. They undermine community.

In this chapter, I propose a view of accountability in which the fundamental aspiration is to create a strong, self-governing, continually improving educational community. This philosophy trusts the local school community and the educators who teach in our schools to be conscientious about their tasks and aims to help them perform their tasks better. It is not naively trusting, so there is some monitoring and a role for governmental agencies. But the primary role of jurisdictions beyond the local school community is to assist more than to coerce. There is a role for standardized testing, but it is not so much to generate incentives through rewards and sanctions as it is to identify students and schools that need help.

THE COMMON VIEW OF ACCOUNTABILITY:
WHY IT IS DYSFUNCTIONAL

I begin with a critique of what I call the "common view." The common view is the view of accountability that underlies legislation such as No Child Left Behind. It is now the focus of the standards paradigm of school reform. It is what people think about when we talk about accountability, hence the label "the common view."

An Accountability Framework

Any view of accountability must answer the following questions:

1. Who is accountable?
2. To whom are they accountable?
3. For what are they accountable?

We can differentiate different views of accountability by how they answer these questions. Moreover, any view of accountability assumes what I call a "theory of action." That is, it assumes a view of why holding people accountable in this particular way is likely to improve educational practice. Finally, any view of accountability will assume norms of legitimate authority. The theory of action and the assumed norms of legitimate authority also serve to distinguish different views of accountability. Here I use this framework to characterize and critique the common view of accountability.

Who is accountable? The common view assumes that those who are accountable are educators, but students also may be viewed as accountable insofar as they must take tests that have consequences for them. That educators are accountable will be a feature of any view. Two things are noteworthy about the common view. The first is that, for the most part, teachers are accountable as employees of their school. The penalties of No Child Left Behind apply to teachers, not as individuals, but only indirectly as they must deal with penalties directed at their schools. Tenure and collective bargaining agreements may to a degree isolate teachers from these penalties unless their schools are closed. To make teachers directly accountable we would need to have pay or tenure depend on test scores. Second, the common view defines educators as public employees. It does this because the common view is essentially a view about how government can monitor and manage a complex educational system so as to control the behavior of subordinates and produce the goals that government desires.

To whom are educators accountable? On the common view educators are accountable primarily to a legislature and its agents. It is legislatures that pass measures requiring accountability, and it is legislatures or their agents that enforce and apply them. Most accountability programs are created by state legislatures or by Congress. Frequently, there is some interaction among different legislative bodies as with No Child Left Behind where states may choose tests and define annual yearly progress within the framework of Congressional legislation. When test results are made public this might assist local communities in holding their schools accountable, but there are few effective means to promote citizen involvement.

For what are educators accountable? The common view holds them accountable for meeting benchmarks most of which are defined by standardized tests on a narrow range of preferred subjects. This is what No Child Left Behind does. Under No Child Left Behind each student is tested in mathematics and reading in every grade from the third to the eighth. They are also tested once in high school. Benchmarks for achievement are set. In a given year a certain percentage of students must be "proficient." The benchmark escalates each year and must be met by each of several demographic groups. Schools are also held accountable for other things, such as graduation rates, but the focus of the common view is on test scores. This is also the form accountability takes when states have high-stakes graduation tests and use results to assess schools as well as students.

What is the theory of action? How is the application of this view supposed to improve education? While No Child Left Behind does mandate remedies for schools failing to meet its benchmarks that might be construed as assistance to schools or students, the real answer to how it is supposed to work is that it generates performance incentives. No Child Left Behind includes requirements that students be tutored by an outside agency, the possibility that students will be given vouchers, being subjected to a school improvement process, and, eventually, closure or reconstitution. There is also an element of public shaming involved. These provisions are perceived as penalties by educators, who seem highly motivated to avoid them. Educators whose schools are in danger of failing to meet some No Child Left Behind benchmark seem to work hard to get their kids to pass tests.

What is the norm of legitimate authority? This view of accountability assumes that the legislature is sovereign. In recent years legislative sovereignty has been exercised so as to increase the actual authority of state legislatures and the U.S. Congress and the bureaucracies they direct and to diminish the authority of local school boards and the autonomy of individual schools. One reason behind the modern accountability movement is the perceived failure of local government to improve the quality of the schools under their direction (Rothstein et al., 2008). I do not propose to challenge the sovereignty of elected legislatures. This is essential to the American conception of a democratic society. But I do propose to question the degree to which operational authority has been assumed by state legislatures and their agents at the expense of those who do the real work of educating our children.

Basic Features of the Common View

These characteristics of the common view suggest several things. First, the kinds of data collected are intended primarily to meet the needs of policy makers, not educators. Educators need immediate and detailed feedback about whether their students and which of their students have learned what they have been recently taught. Policy makers need data that does not require expert judgment to interpret and that can be used to decide questions such as whether a given school is a failing school.

Second, the attempt to design an accountability system that allows policy makers to make global judgments about such things as whether a given school is failing or about the percentage of students who are proficient assumes it is possible to regulate the behavior of employees so as to produce desired outcomes even where the system to be regulated is complex and where many of the goals aimed at are not easily measured. This assumption is far from self-evident.

Third, the use of standardized tests to make summative judgments about schools or teachers imposes costs. Costs increase with the quality of tests. Tests must be accurate and must mean the same thing at different times and places. Good tests test for advanced cognitive skills. To assess these advanced skills, students may be required to write paragraphs or to show their work. These kinds of tests require raters who must be trained and paid. Hence good tests are costly. Because of these costs, the inclination of those who select standardized tests is to purchase them off the shelf rather than create tests that are well aligned to high standards. Often test makers become the real standards setters. Tests used to hold educators accountable are not inevitably good tests.

Fourth, when tests have high stakes for educators, their accuracy as measures of their domain tends to decline. Teachers will tend to teach to the test. This may make test scores go up, but scores on audit tests (different tests that test for the same domain) often do not go up or do not go up at the same rate (Klein, Hamilton, McCaffrey, & Stecher, 2000). This suggests that what students are learning is often a mix of test-taking skills and content that is test specific. It does not follow that their education has been improved. Even rising tests scores are not evidence of good education unless tests are a faithful measure of authentic learning.

Possibilities for Distortion and Corruption

These four features of the common view suggest what Nichols and Berliner (2007) call "Campbell's law" (after its originator, Donald Campbell), which goes like this: "The more any quantitative social indicator is used for social decision making, the more subject it will be to corruption pressures and the more apt it will be to distort and corrupt the social processes it was intended to monitor" (p. 26). Other scholars (Amrein & Berliner, 2002) refer to this as the "uncertainty principle." Hence I must take a closer look as some of the possibilities for distortion and corruption.

Goal displacement. The common view does not attempt to hold educators accountable for all goals. Many Americans believe, for example, that citizenship is an important goal of education (Rothstein, 2008), but systems of accountability rarely hold educators accountable for producing good citizens. Most American believe that students should be able to do research and produce writing showing that they can reason their way through complex issues, but systems of accountability rarely do more than look at the structure of a few paragraphs. Most Americans believe that art and music should have an important place in the education of our children, but systems of accountability rarely hold educators responsible for the ability of our students to create, perform, or appreciate either of these.

We do not hold educators accountable for many of the things we want them to teach our children. We hold them accountable largely for reading and mathematics. The result is that we provide incentives to shift instructional effort toward those subjects for which we test. The curriculum is narrowed. And we should note that a narrowing of the curriculum is most likely to occur in those schools in which children are most likely to fail–in urban schools attended by poor and minority students.

Goal reduction. Goal reduction is the narrowing of goals within a domain for which educators are held accountable. Good tests measure all aspects of the domain they test for. But complex ideas and skills are difficult to measure. They are almost impossible to measure if we must rely on less expensive standardized tests. Thus we can expect test-based accountability systems to produce goal reduction in those subjects for which educators are held accountable since the requirements of affordable testing and of tests that allow easy comparison among schools push us away from the more complex ideas and skills in a given domain and toward those that are most easily measured. Math tests will not test for the ability to use math in solving complex real-world problems. Reading tests will not test for the ability to interpret literature, let alone appreciate it. We want students to be able to research complex topics, draw well-reasoned conclusions from their research, and write persuasively about what they have found and concluded. But this kind of writing is not encouraged by a test-driven accountability system.

Like goal displacement, goal reduction is most likely to occur in those schools that are most at risk for not meeting their accountability benchmarks.

Goal reduction is also likely to take a toll on authentic teaching and learning. Learning that is faithful to its subject matter is best assessed by judging performances–real writing, real research, and real experiments. To the degree that we have expectations that our students will be good at such things, we should doubt the ability of standardized test to test for good education and worry about their potential reductiveness.

Erosion of intrinsic motivation. Teachers are intrinsically motivated when they care about doing a good job. This means that they care about their subjects, seek to teach them with integrity, and enjoy sharing them with their students. And it means that they care about their students and do their best to serve them well. They are motivated by the norms of their profession, and they care about their school communities. They take pride in their work, and the success of their school and their students is a source of pleasure and pride.

The imposition of external incentives tends to erode the commitment to internalized norms. Thomas Sergiovanni (1992) tells this story: Once there was a school whose teachers generally arrived early and left late, often staying late to improve their instruction or to work with students. They cared about their work and put in the time required to do it well. Yet a few did not. They left school as soon as they were able. In order to deal with these few slackers, the principal created a rule. Teachers were required to stay until a certain time, not as late as most already stayed, but later than the few usually left. Soon almost all of the teachers left at this time.

Motivation is a social product. It is influenced by institutional body language. When an institution's leaders and its practices convey a sense that people are trusted and when people are devoted to the goals of their community, most people will respond by putting in the time and effort required to do a good job. When an institution emphasizes rules and compliance and enforces rules with rewards or punishments, people may respond with compliance, but their commitment to their task will erode. When an institution's every action says "get those scores up or else," internal motivation will be difficult to maintain.

People who are dealt with on the assumption that their behavior is motivated largely by calculations of personal benefit and who feel distrusted will come to have their behavior determined largely by calculations of personal benefits. They will come to fulfill the expectations of this prophecy of distrust. Incentives easily create an alienated culture in which professionals are transformed into mere employees, feel unappreciated and disrespected, do only what is required or what is effectively enforced, and care little for the outcomes schools aim to produce.

The common view of accountability thus has a tendency to alter the goals and motivation of educators away from working to provide a good education and toward meeting benchmarks and responding to incentives. Internalized norms rooted in a deep understanding of subject matter, the foundational purposes of education, a professional culture, and the love of students are eroded. Imperfect measures come to define success; effort becomes motivated by calculations of self interest.

Gaming the system. By "gaming the system," I mean finding ways to meet prescribed benchmarks that do not actually serve the goals that these benchmarks are supposed to measure. People who are subject to external incentives will make decisions based on calculations of how their behavior affects their personal welfare. Thus a system that works on incentives must be sure that its incentives reward only desired behaviors and do not reward dysfunctional behavior. Otherwise people will find ways to game the system. People are often able to game the system when the system is complex and when the goals are subjective.

The most obvious example of gaming is outright fraud–providing students the answers to test questions, for example. There are many other examples: Teaching to the test with no consideration of the degree to which the test expresses an adequate conception of the subject matter is a form of gaming. Substituting test preparation and rote learning for inquiry and reflection is a form of gaming. Focusing resources on students who are "on the bubble" and ignoring those who are sure to pass or sure to fail is a form of gaming. Taking resources from areas of instruction not tested and placing them in areas where there is a test without consideration of student need is a form of gaming. Redefining the meaning of a passing score so as to achieve a politically acceptable pass rate is a form of gaming. Encouraging students to drop out or misclassifying them so that underperforming students do not take the tests on which the school is to be judged is a form of gaming. It is hard to say how common these forms of gaming are, but they seem common enough (Nichols & Berliner, 2007a; Rothstein et al., 2008).

Erosion of the language of standards. One of the more pernicious and subtle consequences of the common view is its corruption of the language we use to talk about such ideas as rigor and excellence. The very concept of a standard is changed and terms that depend on it are redefined as well.

Everyone thinks that high standards are good things in some sense. But what exactly is a standard? Consider two potential meanings of the idea of a *standard*. I call them "standards as benchmarks," and "standards as criteria of excellence."

The common view of accountability generally sees standards as benchmarks, as answers to the question "What do we want students to know and to be able to do?" When we have created an adequate list of such standards, we have the makings of a curriculum. We can then create tests that are aligned with these content standards. When we have done this, we can make a judgment as to how many right answers on a given test constitute an acceptable grasp of the subject. When we have done this, we have created a benchmark for individual achievement. We can then aggregate these scores so that we can have benchmarks for schools, school systems, and even states. We have high standards when the passing score is high: 65 is higher than 55, hence better, more rigorous. A school that has more students with 65s than another school is more excellent, its programs are more rigorous.

Standards as criteria of excellence are importantly different. Imagine that you have fallen into a conference of mathematicians. You have gone out in the evening with a couple of them to have dinner. They are talking about one of their number whom they claim is a first-rate mathematician. What do you imagine they would say? Here are some possibilities: "Jones is an excellent mathematician. The new proof she demonstrated in her paper was highly original. She did more than prove the theorem she set out to prove; she did it in a way that was not only rigorous, but was positively elegant. The way she reduced the number of steps in the proof from previous attempts was not only ingenious, but it generated new insights into the problem." Here the standards used to judge mathematicians and their work are originality, rigor of proof and argument, elegance, consistency, explanatory power, and insightfulness.

Or imagine a group of poets discussing a new poem. Listen again: "Smith's poem was inspired. It combined a beauty of language with a precision of phrasing and an economy of words. Every word was carefully chosen and exactly right. When I finished with it, I had achieved a new insight into the topic Smith wrote about." Here elegance of form, consistency, beauty, economy of language, precision, and originality are the standards used to judge the excellence of poets and their work.

The difference between these two kinds of standards is not the difference between the appraisal of professional work and the appraisal of public school students. The example of Ms. S. from Chapter 3 will illustrate. Her focus in getting us to examine the proof that $1 = 0$ was on showing us what counted in mathematics. She also wanted us to experience the joy of problem solving. Thus in the earliest days of elementary algebra we were introduced to the demands of mathematics for coherence and consistency, its resistance to the paradoxical, and its rejection of the contradictory. Often there was a kind of "gee, golly whiz" air about what we were discovering–perhaps the ninth-grade equivalent of awe.

These three examples furnish the following characteristics of standards as criteria of excellence or simply "standards of excellence":

1. Standards of excellence are employed to judge the quality of performances, but in a way that has little to do with reaching test-defined benchmarks. These standards have to do with the rigor of argument or the beauty of language.
2. Standards of excellence are things to be internalized. This is part of normation. Standards are norms.
3. The internalization of standards of excellence is a prerequisite of excellence in performance. One who has not internalized the standards of some area does not know what a good performance is.
4. Standards of excellence can be applied to the evaluation of performances only by those with sufficient expertise.
5. Standards of excellence connect learning to belonging. Standards are created, nurtured, and transmitted by the cooperative and collegial activities of communities–groups of mathematicians, scientists, artists, athletes, and craftspeople. To have high standards is to affiliate with these communities.
6. Standards of excellence are transformative. When people have internalized them, they are able to experience the world in new ways and what they value has changed in them.
7. The mastery of standards of excellence enhances the quality of experience. One is not only enabled to see the world differently but to enjoy it in new ways.

This conception of standards as criteria of excellence is essential to any adequate conception of a good education. It is central to the idea of normation. Internalizing standards helps to constitute community by shaping what students value and care about. When we engage in authentic teaching and authentic assessment, we appeal to this idea of what standards are, and we use this notion to define rigor and excellence. But the common view of accountability teaches us that standards are lists of what we want kids to know and be able to do–the kinds of things we can use to create tests and define benchmarks. And it teaches us that we should define rigor and excellence in terms of the numbers of children who get certain predefined percentages of answers right on these tests.

This alteration of the meaning of terms such as *standards, excellence*, and *rigor* is not a trivial matter. It influences how we talk, how we think, and what we see. It predisposes us to think of education as a process that will increase test scores and not as a process that will enable students to show excellence in what they do. The kinds of aspirations that are important to authentic teaching will become unintelligible to us if we think of standards as benchmarks because we will have lost even the means to articulate them.

Changes in authority relations, sense of community, and workplace conditions. In the view of democratic governance I described in Chapter 5, the local school aspires to be a polity. Part of what it means to be a polity is that those who are associated together in a school have agreed to a kind of social contract that spells out the school's distinctive educational philosophy and program. The social contract also spells out the nature of governance. While the details of this can vary, there are a couple of essential features: The first is that there should be a collegium. The second is that there should be institutions and practices that encourage the participation of all citizens of the school community in deliberations about matters of common concern. These essential features have three fundamental purposes: (1) They encourage the community to take responsibility for its educational program; (2) they help create a sense of community; (3) they help to create a nonalienating workplace.

These are all elements of good schools. Good schools are schools where teachers work together to plan and evaluate programs and to help one another and where the involvement of parents and students is valued. They are, as Chubb notes in the quote at the beginning of this chapter, schools that have a mission and take responsibility for it. Schools that must emphasize raising test scores are less likely to have a mission for which they take responsibility.

When teachers form a collegium and where parents are involved, their cooperative activities are community constituting. Their dialogue and their cooperation help reinforce a sense of shared purpose and shared commitment. Trust is created. And when these things exist, they create the kind of solidarity that makes the processes of deliberation and cooperation easier. This kind of shared effort helps to create a non-alienating workplace and a culture of success. People find working together both useful and rewarding. Most importantly, they experience a sense of ownership over their work and their goals. But the common view of accountability tends to undermine all of this.

Consider a passage from New York State's *A New Compact for Learning* (1994):

> This is the essence of the New Compact for Learning: that schools and school districts exercise initiative to make what changes may be needed to bring about the learning results we all desire. In a new relationship between the State and

localities, the State defines more precisely what is to be learned, and local teachers, administrators, and boards of education have more freedom to decide how such learning is to occur. (p. 10)

Here New York proposes a division of labor between the state and the local districts and schools. The state will determine the goals and set the standards and the local district and local schools will have more freedom to implement them. This division of labor was much influenced by research into effective schools (Edmonds, 1979) and the argument that good schools have significant autonomy and other organizational characteristics that are reasonably similar to the ones I have associated with democratic schools. Thus New York's proposal is, in effect, to wed standards-based reform and site-based management.

A New Compact was written at a time when the primary emphasis of the standards movement was the creation of an educational system rather than accountability. Given this, the idea that local schools would have more autonomy to implement their educational programs is at least plausible. Nevertheless, the state's message to educators might be paraphrased, "You are free to do what we tell you however you want." This is not the kind of freedom required to create and pursue a shared educational project.

The division of labor proposed is also naive. When states and large districts take on the responsibility to ensure better schools and hold them accountable, the freedom that educators are supposed to have to develop their own implementation strategies is not likely to last much past the first negative reports about test scores. In fact, states and districts have tended to follow their ventures into standard setting with inquiries into best practice and often generate conflicting mandates and regulations of all sorts. This has been especially true of urban schools (Anyon, 1997).

The common view undermines local goal setting. It substitutes a standardized curriculum for one responsive to local needs, conditions, and preferences. It substitutes a regime of compliance for one emphasizing local deliberation and local responsibility taking. And it substitutes a hierarchical authority structure where each level is responsible to see to it that subordinates do what is required to raise test scores and meet benchmarks. It undermines intrinsic motivation and ownership of programs. In doing these things, it makes it difficult for the school to be a polity, it undermines the deliberative and cooperative processes that create community, and it creates an alienated workplace.

Evidence-based decision making. There has been much recent talk about evidence-based decision making. A former associate of mine who was the director of research for a large school district was fond of saying, "In God we trust, everyone else brings data." This is a good line. But what kinds of data are useful for the improvement of instruction?

The kinds of data generated by the common view are of poor quality for this purpose. They are, in the jargon of assessment, largely summative, not formative. They provide low-quality and untimely feedback to educators about the progress of individual students and almost no feedback to students.

What teachers need are good tests that are given reasonably often and that provide timely information on whether their students have learned what they have been recently taught. Such tests are characteristically created by the teachers. In many cases what we want are not tests, but "performances." We want to encourage students to write, to do experiments, to play music and create art, to research important topics and report their results. Tests and performances of this sort tell teachers whether their students have learned what they have been taught, whether they can exhibit the excellences that lead to the goods internal to the practice they seek to master. They encourage authentic teaching and express authentic learning. They permit teachers to review what has not been well learned and to adjust their practice to improve results. And they enable teacher feedback to students. Authentic learning requires feedback. Performances must be critiqued. Teachers can comment on reports and essays. They can critique arguments. The results of standardized tests do little of this.

It might be argued that the common view provides incentives to educators to make more extensive use of the kinds of tests and performance evaluations I have recommended. Perhaps the tests required by the common view do not do much more than provide an end-of-year summary judgment of whether students are learning. At the same time, if the kind of tests and evaluations of performances I have recommended are part of good educational practice, then they are more likely to be adopted because of the testing required by the common view.

This is not implausible, but I think it is doubtful. The tests employed for accountability on the common view might provide teachers with an incentive to use the assessment practices most likely to facilitate authentic learning if these tests measured authentic learning. But they do not. What they are likely to encourage teachers to do is to make more extensive use of tests that are similar to the ones that are used to define the benchmarks on which they or their school will be judged. When they can get them, teachers will spend time going over released versions of those tests. This is what regularly happens in New York State with the Regents Exams. The common view is likely to result in the substitution of test prep for the kinds of timely assessment of authentic learning that good education requires.

The common view of accountability thus has much about it that is likely to undermine authentic teaching and learning. It does not support a process of continued improvement. If, not being God, we must bring data, it would be nice if the data we brought were useful for improving instruction. The data generated by the common view are not.

ACCOUNTABILITY FOR COMMUNITY

At the beginning of the chapter I took note of a new charter school being opened in Ithaca New York. This school proposed to emphasize ecology, environmental issues, and sustainability. What kind of accountability would help this new school flourish? What should accountability be like in schools that are communities? Implicit in the argument of this chapter are some "standards" for a form of accountability that enables community and promotes school improvement.

1. Accountability should primarily be accountability to the community and to professional standards, especially those that define authentic learning. It should be only secondarily accountability to an educational bureaucracy or a legislature and its agents.
2. Accountability should enhance community, local responsibility, and local governance. Accountability should contribute to an environment in which those who do the work of educating take responsibility for the quality and effectiveness of their work–an environment that creates a sense of ownership for educational programs within the community. Democratic localism should not be undermined. Accountability should not be alienating.
3. Educational goals should be chosen prior to and independently of the selection of the instruments of accountability. Goals should be chosen because they are what we want schools to accomplish and because there are good reasons for them. They should not be chosen because they are easily measured, quantified, or satisfy the needs of policy makers.
4. Accountability should encourage authentic teaching and learning.
5. All goals should be assessed. It is especially important that those goals that are distinctive to a school's shared educational project be assessed.
6. Goals should be assessed in ways that are appropriate to their character. When goals involve capacities that are best expressed through performances, they should be assessed by the observations of performances that are as close as is feasible to the normal expression of these capacities.
7. Goals should not be assessed in ways that distort the curriculum or teaching.
8. Accountability should aim to inform the community and provide evidence that is relevant to instructional improvement.
9. Accountability should aim to assist rather than to coerce. An

acceptable view of accountability should aim first of all to improve education by providing information useful to those who do the work of educating concerning how instruction can be improved. It should be formative rather than summative.

10. Accountability schemes should not have perverse incentives. They should not give an incentive for gaming.

What vision of accountability meets these criteria? What vision might help New Roots to flourish? I suggested earlier in this chapter that views of accountability can be defined by answers to three questions. Here is my alternative to the common view.

Who is accountable? Educators are accountable. But they are not accountable as employees. They are accountable as members of a collegium and as community members.

To whom are educators accountable? Educators are accountable primarily to the school community, to students and their families, and to professional communities concerning teaching authentically and with integrity.

For what are educators accountable? They are accountable to effectively provide the educational program required by the school's shared educational program and spelled out in its social contract.

Accountability begins with the school's shared educational project and its social contract. These are the initial means that the school uses to constitute a community. Those who create the school find a way to effectively communicate the school's educational philosophy. They describe their goals and their educational program. They explain how the school goes about pursuing its goals. Teachers agree to teach in a school because they share its vision, and families elect to send their children to a school because they share its vision. The members of the community agree that this is what they want, and they agree to do their part and fulfill their commitments. Accountability is accountability of each to all. It is the way in which the community assures itself that all are doing their part, and it is the means by which school improvement is sought.

The first task in creating and implementing a vision of accountability is thus to achieve clarity about the goals of the school. Then we ask two questions: "How will we know that we are addressing all of our goals?" and "How will we know that all kids are learning what we are trying to teach them?" Answering these questions requires that schools develop a view about the kinds of evidence they will collect and a systematic program to collect it and use it. The evidence may be test results or portfolios of work. It is important that student work be discussed and questions be asked about whether students are mastering the intellectual skills they need to be good citizens and to make competent decisions about their own lives. It may require inquiry about what has happened to graduates: Have they gone to college? Are they active in their communities? It may require discussions about how effective programs are and how they shape aspirations and about whether they are transformative.

Accountability has two main functions. First, it informs the school community about how the school is doing. Thus a plan for accountability includes a view about how progress is communicated to the community and includes opportunity to discuss results. Second, it is the primary means whereby the school seeks to improve itself. Collecting appropriate evidence, discussing it, and evaluating it need to be a part of how the collegium does its business and its planning.

The deliberations of the collegium should be conducted by appealing to informed standards of good work and excellence. They are the primary ways in which a professional culture is established and maintained. Conscientious discussions among professionals are an important means whereby professional standards are learned and internalized. What goes on among teachers is crucial to a good and effective educational community. If teachers are cynical, self-centered, or feel defeated, new teachers will catch their vices. If teachers collaborate, and if important matters are discussed in a professional way, new teachers will catch their virtues. A good program for accountability makes the community self-correcting and self-disciplining. Leadership is, perhaps, most crucial here. Leaders set the tone for their communities. A good leader holds the members of the community to their responsibilities and tends to the process.

The emphasis is thus on how the community can be made accountable to itself. A well-thought-through and conscientiously executed system of accountability can be the basis of school improvement and can be community constituting. It can help create ownership of the school's shared educational project and of its programs. Ownership of what one does, acting because this is what one wishes to do, and having what one wants to do shaped by others through cooperative effort and respectful discussion are key; indeed, they are the meaning of a nonalienating workplace.

What is the role of those legislatures that govern schools? The first role of the school district and the state is to enforce the conditions of the social contract. When a school is created through a contract with its district or other agency, it makes certain promises. When it hires teachers, promises are made to them. When families send their children to a school, they agree to an educational program because it is viewed as best for their children; as a result, promises are made to them. It is the responsibility of government to make policies that ensure that the promises made serve the public interest and that schools deliver on what they promise to do.

This requires monitoring. Monitoring can be accomplished by visitations and by some testing. When schools have a good accountability program, they should be able to produce documentation that external agencies can inspect, evaluate, and pass judgment on. Does this put pressure on schools? Of course. While I believe that the workplace is a powerful tool of socialization and that once a good workplace is established people will internalize its norms, I also believe that people are not saints. They will make mistakes, they will from time to time behave badly and selfishly, and they will squabble. When they are incompetent or behave badly, they harm children. There needs to be someone to notice and to act. We should base a system of accountability on the assumption that most of the time most educators will behave well and professionally when they work in a school with good leadership and a healthy professional culture, but we cannot base a system of accountability on a naive view about human perfectibility. People are people.

There is a role for standardized tests. I would suggest that students be tested largely for basic skills and at important transitional points. We can test for whether students can read and do mathematics. These skills are foundational. So let us monitor how kids are doing as they move from elementary school to middle school (or junior high), and as they move on to high school.

We need early identification of students whose basic skills, especially reading, need remediation. Schools can then take steps to help them. When schools have a great many of these students, they need help. Districts and states should take steps to help such schools. Helping needs to begin with an inquiry into the nature of the problem and into remedies and resources that are needed to address the matter. Inspection, investigation, and discussion are the order of the day.

A few schools and a few teachers may prove recalcitrant or hopeless. Districts should be willing to close persistently failing schools and fire incompetent teachers. Moreover, I would have a fairly long probationary period before tenure was given and fairly rigorous requirements for getting it. But the district's primary orientation to schools is to help, not coerce. Effective monitoring may occasionally be threatening, but its fundamental point is not to erect incentives or sanctions. It is to discover and remediate problems.

Finally, the kind of accountability I have recommended for schools that wish to be communities is hard and time-consuming. Districts may help here, too. They can provide models, instruments, professional development, and consultants. They can help organize schools into consortia where ideas can be shared.

These kinds of things require resources and commitment. But first and foremost they require a vision of accountability that emphasizes the creation of strong educational communities. The key is to find ways to encourage educators to take responsibility for their own work and to take collective responsibility for the success of their schools. The common view leads to strategies that do just the opposite. They make educators responsible to meet benchmarks that they have no role in setting and that may have little connection to the kind of educational program that they believe is a good program. They provide numerous perverse incentives, destroy commitment, and create alienating workplaces. They are anticommunity and miseducative. We need views of accountability that create community.

If Wishes Were Fishes

*Conclusions, Doubts,
and the Big Picture*

The best things in life aren't things.
–Bumper sticker

I said at the outset of this book that three aphorisms were the key ideas of this book and the key to educational reform:

Authentic learning is an act of affiliation.
We are all in this together.
Alienation is the problem; community is the cure.

Where has the development of these ideas taken us?

A FEW CONCLUSIONS AND SOME DOUBTS

In healthy cultures children and adolescents want to master the ideas and skills that are important to being recognized as respected adults in their culture. They see themselves as apprentice adults. Learning begins with the bonds between adults and children. Children speak the language of their parents and their immediate communities. They come to like the same foods and worship the same gods. They internalize the values, commitments, and understandings of their caregivers and their communities. As they do these things, they take on the characteristics and outlook of the adults whose esteem and recognition they value. Their membership in their communities becomes less dependent on their parentage, less dependent on "natural affections," and more dependent on shared values, beliefs, and identities. Strong communities are important to this process of normation. Strong communities will not turn children into angels, overcome the effects of poverty, repeal the recalcitrance of human nature, or turn adolescents into saints–but strong communities make good education possible.

In advanced liberal democratic and capitalist societies this "way of things" does not always work well. Modernity has weakened community. As children grow, their socialization is accomplished through many diverse and partial communities. Commitment to the values of these communities is weak. There are many competing influences, sometimes of doubtful worth. The intergenerational transfer of norms that good education requires often does not work well in schools largely because schools reflect the societies that create them.

It works even less well as adolescents move into high schools. Modern high schools are often incoherent. They lack coherent shared values and a shared educational program. For many children they may seem to express the values of someone else's culture and devalue their own. And they can be anonymous, alienating, and bureaucratic in ways that disrupt the connection between adults and children on which normation depends. If we want to reform them, we need to find ways to make them into good communities where the process of normation works.

Yet good school communities should not create the "bads" of community. We are, after all, a liberal democratic society where it is important to respect and value diversity. And we learn from diverse others. The diversity of our society is an educational plus, not a liability. One role of the modern high school is to affirm this pluralism. A good school is not one with a ruling doctrine or a dominant identity. It is a marketplace of ideas where such truth as is to be found is sought from a multiplicity of voices. The role of the high school is not so much to affirm the culture or convictions of parents and their particular communities, but to question them and permit students to find their own truth and their own path.

Do we want schools to be places where students find their own path and their own truth? Yes and no. There is much in this story of diversity to affirm. The solution to creating schools that are communities is not to be found in affirming *"the* truth" or *"the* way" so that institutional coherence can be had.

Yet if schools are to educate well, they must be able to do the work of normation. They must be communities that are strong enough to effectively transmit the values that underlie what they are trying to teach. After all, a real marketplace of ideas is possible only where people care about ideas and where they possess the knowledge and skills to assess them. Without authoritative commitment to such ideals a diversity of ideas and identities leads to a shouting match, not to the collective pursuit of truth.

The diversity that liberals prize is not what undermines community. What undermines community is a certain kind of individualism–one rooted in YOYO ("You're on your own") rather than WITT ("We're in this together"). The modern high school–and to an increasing degree middle schools and elementary schools as well–is devoted to the proposition that the fundamental role of schooling is to provide children the tools they need for individual success in the marketplace. The hidden curriculum of the modern school does not tell students to value ideas and the pursuit of truth. It tells them that the good life consists of money, power, attractiveness, and stuff. Its central norm, equality of opportunity, aims at fair competition, but we are not thoughtful about what we teach our children to compete for.

Part of this story about the role of schooling must be affirmed. We do, should, and must teach subjects that are of economic value in schools; and so long as prized and scarce positions in higher education and good jobs are allocated on the basis of educational success, equal opportunity must be part of the story about schooling. What undermines community is the fact that this story seems increasingly to be the only one that counts. What other stories are there to tell? There are two.

The first story emphasizes that the things we teach are valuable for reasons other than that they are the means of economic competition and productivity. They are worthwhile because they enhance our ability to appreciate experience, because they help make us wise, and because they help create good citizens and good friends.

We can only create good educational communities when we affirm what MacIntyre (1981) calls the "goods internal to practices." When children study science to get into a good college, other students are their competition. When they study science because they want to understand how the universe works or how to improve the human condition, others are potential collaborators in a common project. When they study mathematics or literature of history with someone like Ms. S.–someone who cares about the goods internal to practices and who cares about kids enough to want to share these goods–then community is formed. Students are engaged in a common project from which all can benefit. They pursue common goods. I suspect that they will also turn out to be more productive as a result.

What follows is that we create community in schools by valuing our intellectual heritages; that is, we value the project of sharing with the next generation the best that our diverse cultures have produced–along with their debates about what is really best. This is central to what I have called authentic teaching. Not to do this is to lie about the subjects we teach.

A second story we need to tell about schools is the story about democratic community. This requires more than that we teach the virtues of voting and electoral participation. It requires that the school be a kind of polity–a place where all are equally valued, where the test of community is how we care for the weakest members, where common goods are collectively and cooperatively pursued, and where the views of all are attended to. It requires a sense of WITT.

Good school communities that are communities of practice and democratic communities are neither too thick nor too thin. They help create the goods of community–a sense of belonging, friendship, shared values, and shared identities–and they encourage the normation that is essential to good education. But they do not produce the "bads" of community–parochialism, indoctrination, intolerance. Good educational communities may have a curricular focus or theme, but they are otherwise inclusive. They include people of diverse faiths, races, and ethnicities. To have such inclusive communities, we need to defend the worth of the goods internal to the practices we teach and to defend democratic community. We need to understand the difference between an education that enriches life and one that seeks merely to make us rich.

And we need schools with institutional characteristics that allow us to succeed on these aspirations. That it is a bad idea to herd adolescents into large, anonymous, and bureaucratic institutions seems to me to be as close to a no-brainer as anything I can think of in education. And this is an especially bad idea for the poor and minority youth who often attend large, failing urban schools. Such institutions are inconsistent with the developmental needs of adolescents and the requirements of a good education. They deny youth a sense of belonging as junior members of the adult world, and they do not inspire them to value the goods that are internal to the education adults struggle to provide. Indeed, they are almost perfectly designed to reinforce the influence of peers and diminish the influence of adults.

I find it remarkable that we have created so many such schools. Even more astonishing is the fact that we did this (and continue to do it 30 years later) against the advice of a well-reasoned and well-researched presidential report, *Youth: Transition to Adulthood* (Coleman, 1974), that recognized alienation and age segregation as central educational problems and suggested plausible steps to cure them. But we preferred the analysis and the solutions of another presidential report, *A Nation at Risk* (National Commission on Excellence in Education, 1983), that appeared a decade later. We set ourselves on the path that led to No Child Left Behind, we committed ourselves to a reform agenda that valued human capital formation and little else, and we initiated the state versus market debate that has dominated educational reform. That, after more than 2 decades, we have gotten little from the various waves of educational reform in the wake of *A Nation at Risk* has not seemed to many policy makers to be a reason why we should examine our core assumptions about school reform. Even in the wake of the disaster that No Child Left Behind has become, many think it can be fixed by more and better tests and more and better accountability. I see no hope for our schools here.

What kinds of schools do we need? We need schools that focus on what is required to enrich lives more than on what is required to create successful employees and consumers. We need schools that care about truth, goodness, and beauty, not just about higher test scores. We need schools that surround kids with caring and accomplished adults, schools that have social structures and practices in which these adults are formative influences on kids' lives. We need schools where the need for belonging is satisfied by initiating students into communities of practice and into democratic communities. We need schools that are coherent enough to allow them to be energized by a shared commitment to the school's project rather than by compliance to rules, schools with a mission where we can trust other members of the community to do what serves that mission, schools where adults value ideas and kids and where kids see this and respond.

We are most likely to be able to create these schools if we have schools that are small, but we will not get such schools merely by creating small schools. Small schools can create the conditions for community formation, but community does not just happen. It needs to be thought about, planned for, created, and cared for. Educational community requires a worthy shared vision and capable people committed to carrying it out.

Can we create such schools? The small schools movement offers hope. Small schools can create the social conditions under which community becomes possible. And many small schools advocates have the right idea about community and about good educating. The Coalition of Essential Schools has educational commitments that are on the side of the angels here and has been an effective advocate for small schools.

But there are reasons for concern. Some advocates of small schools seem overly individualistic in their views, seeing personalization as more about individualized instruction or reducing it to nothing more than strong affective relations between students and adults. They lack a vision of community formation. Often when large districts attempt to scale up small schools, they seem to think that if they just create small schools good things will happen. They lose sight of what else is required.

The main problem however is that much in modern culture is not supportive. We have a culture with some profoundly anti-intellectual tendencies. Our political culture often degrades intellect as elitist. It is almost un-American to be smart and well educated. Some religious groups have made the capacity to disregard or distort evidence into a spiritual virtue. They encourage ignorance and hypocrisy. And there are many competing influences. I am a lover of many varieties of music and sport, but there is much in the culture of modern music and athletics that is morally toxic.

Our culture tends to value intellect only instrumentally. Ideas are seen largely as commodities. They are productive resources and the means of economic competition. But we do not seem to value intellect because it makes us better people, better citizens, or transforms us so that we are able to enjoy experience more. Indeed, we are often suspicious of such ideals because they may seem illiberal as well as elitist. We do not have a commitment to a democratic culture that is, to borrow a phrase from Benjamin Barber (1992), "an aristocracy of everyone."

Nor does our culture value the collective pursuit of common goods. We have been told by several generations of politicians now that government is the problem, not the solution. We have been taught to think of taxes, not as money we provide to see to the common good, but as a kind of theft on the part of a government that takes our money and wastes it often for the benefit of the undeserving poor. Our elites tend not to think of their careers as making a social contribution by creating products that make our lives better. Indeed, the (alleged) "best and the brightest" seem increasingly to want to enrich themselves by finding ever more creative ways to gamble with other people's money, and they measure their success by having more than others and more than they can possibly use. We are a society where YOYO is well ahead of WITT. We transfer these attitudes to education and to our children.

This state of affairs creates a dilemma for those of us of liberal democratic inclination. To some extent, we Americans have the schools we deserve. Our schools reflect entrenched values. A culture that is based on possessive individualism should not expect its schools to produce elites who are civic minded. A culture that does not value the life of the mind and that is more concerned for fair competition than democratic community should not expect to have schools to which intellectual and democratic community are central. Educators who want such schools will be sailing into a stiff wind.

So far as educational reform is concerned, we have even corrupted the language in which the ideals of a good education can be articulated. When we speak of the need for rigor or excellence now, what is heard is a demand for higher test scores and more accountability, not for schools where ideas are valued and excellence is shown through performance. When we speak of standards, we think about test-defined benchmarks, not of the human excellences that require education to cultivate. It is hard to see how we can create good schools when we are robbed even of the language in which we can discuss them.

Perhaps this is too pessimistic. We do have many good schools. And we have many dedicated educators who have created them. Many of these schools are small schools, and in many places we are trying to scale them up.

But we are not doing a great job in scaling up the kind of vision that has made small schools good schools and strong communities. People who have created good small schools have been motivated by a desire to create an education that reflects their vision. When they have succeeded, they have succeeded because they have created schools that have attracted capable and energetic individuals who share their vision and because they have recruited students (or their parents) who valued the kind of education they wanted to provide. They did not succeed because of the vision of policy makers or because of significant institutional support. They succeeded because they were able to find and defend a space for their vision. They have succeeded in sailing against the wind.

Schools that are strong communities and good small schools are, I suspect, unlikely to happen merely because policy makers catch a vision for small schools, provide the resources for them, and create the institutional support they require. Policy makers are likely to view small schools as though they were big schools with fewer students. They may help to create many new small schools, but they may also regulate the life from them or staff them with people who lack a vision for the enterprise or the training and capacity to carry it out. They may see them as ways to improve test scores and will quickly abandon them if test scores do not improve.

One reason why it is so important to have clarity of vision for small schools as strong communities is to prevent this kind of domestication. I do not believe that good schools are likely to be created from the top because policy makers catch the vision. They will, to be sure, require a policy environment that is supportive. But they will need to be created by committed people with a vision and a sense of mission, people who have already had experience with good small schools and who are willing to share their vision and expertise with others. We need institutional practices that encourage this pioneering spirit, ones that develop networks and that allow new schools to experiment and grow.

While I think that there is a strong moral imperative to reform schools, I also believe that we should scale up small schools with caution. Crash efforts will result in many small schools with the hope that if we create them something good will happen. The staff will not be able to plan and will not be socialized to the educational commitments of those who have succeeded. Policy will be in the hands of those who do not get it. We will not get good schools by wishing and casting our net into the sea. Wishes are not fishes.

Joe Nathan (2008), a strong advocate of small schools, quotes some correspondence from two less optimistic scholars, Michael McPherson and Harry Brighouse, about scaling up small schools:

> One thing that is striking about detailed discussions of particular school experiences is the centrality of leadership, and the fact that small schools have often given leaders much more power than they usually have in big schools, enabling them better to get the teachers . . . that they want. To the extent that this increased flexibility improves productivity it is scalable up, but to the extent that

it just allows . . . schools to act as magnets for talented teachers and administrators and sympathetic parents, it is not. (p. 18)

This raises a serious concern, but I think it miscasts it. I have argued that good small schools are best created by giving freedom to people with a vision to create a school. If the schools they create succeed because they are able to cream the best from a limited talent pool of teachers, then this places great constraints on their scalability. No educational reform can succeed in scaling up if it depends on a steady stream of people of above average ability and dedication.

The underlying assumption of this concern is that the supply of talented and committed teachers is fixed and limited and that small schools are only able to succeed in virtue of their ability to outcompete other schools for this limited supply. This may be wrong in two ways. First, it does not take into account the possibility that good schools with a supportive culture and unburdened by excessive regulations might serve to bring good new teachers into the educational system. Second, it does not take into account that the quality of current teachers may be improved by schools that value them, create a positive, supportive, and educative culture, and provide the networking and training required for them to come to understand and pursue a new vision.

I am hopeful that we can succeed in both ways. We need to make teaching a more attractive field. Small schools can help here simply because teachers like to work in them. We need to create programs to train people to function in small schools that are strong communities. But we also need to learn how to build on success. This requires networking where successful creators of small schools work intensively with people who wish to create them over sustained periods of time.

Finally, the kinds of reform I have advocated require commitment to and advocacy for a coherent agenda, one where the core values are intellectual community and democratic community. Apart from such advocacy, those who have power to make policy will continue to act on the assumptions of old reform models and see small schools as little more than a strategy to raise test scores. Undoubtedly, we will create more small schools, but we may create them without doing what is required to make them strong communities. We may throw together people who do not share a common vision and ask them to create a school over the summer. We may ask for authentic teaching but assess new schools using standardized tests. Then we will find that these new schools are not much better than the schools they replace. The small schools movement will turn out to be another flash in the pan, another failed experiment. Sometimes in education we seem to believe that anything worth doing is worth doing badly.

Perhaps we can do better. Doing better requires that we keep our eye on the prize and that we advocate for policies that implement a coherent vision.

SILVER BULLETS AND THE BIG PICTURE

There are no silver bullets to be found in small schools that are strong communities. These reforms, no matter how energetically carried out, are not going to transform urban schools dramatically. They are not, by themselves, going to cure the rather large achievement gaps that plague our society. One does not subject children to poverty, discrimination, and toxic environments and expect to have schools undo the consequences, no matter how good and how nurturing these schools are.

Real educational reform requires more than better schools. It requires a context in which good schools can succeed. It requires such things as better health care, universal preschool, housing stabilization, and a host of other programs that can create decent lives and stable communities for all our children.

An emphasis on community can play a role here. A healthy society has stable and educative communities, not just stable and educative schools. WITT is affirmed over YOYO, the weakest are cared for, possessive individualism is not the default ethic, and common goods are created and collectively pursued. This is not just an ethic for schools. It is an ethic for our social life generally.

Healthy societies need a robust civil society. In a robust civil society people are shaped by belonging–belonging to civic organizations, community choirs, congregations, and, to use an overworked illustration, bowling leagues (Putnam, 1995). Barker and Gump (1964), in their work on small rural schools, note the positive formative influence of participation on small communities. The small town in which I live has a good school where kids are cared for and well educated. It also has a robust civic life. Everyone seems to be on the board of something. People ski in ski clubs and snowmobile in snowmobile clubs. There are numerous community groups. People work together for the benefit of their community. There is trust. This helps to produce a town where there is virtually no crime and where people come to each other's aid when there is an emergency or a tragedy. Money is collected, clothing distributed, strangers show up with casseroles.

But my town is a community of place. Civil society is harder in urban areas. Just as we need to work at community in urban schools, we need to work at community in urban neighborhoods.

Ultimately, successful urban schools will be the product of successful urban communities. We in America have allowed urban areas to decay. We have not attended to civil society. We have allowed YOYO to triumph over WITT. We have created a plutocracy more than a democracy. We value the needs of the few over those of the many. The schools we have reflect the values we have. But we do not have the schools our children need. A more intentional care for community in our schools, if not a silver bullet, is still an important step forward.

References

Ackerman, B. (1980). *Social justice in the liberal state.* New Haven, CT: Yale University Press.

Amrein, A. L., & Berliner, D. C. (2002). High-stakes testing, uncertainty, and student learning. *Education Policy Analysis Archives 10*(18). Retrieved August 25, 2009, from http://epaa.asu.edu/epaa/v10n18

Anyon, J. (1997). *Ghetto schooling: A political economy of urban educational reform.* New York: Teachers College Press.

Apple, M., & Beane, J. (Eds.). (1995). *Democratic schools.* Alexandria, VA: ASCD.

Aristotle. (1941). Nicomachean ethics (W.D. Ross, Trans.). In R. McKeon (Ed.), *The basic works of Aristotle.* New York: Random House.

Arons, S. (1997). *Short route to chaos.* Amherst: University of Massachusetts Press.

Barber, B. (1992). *An aristocracy of everyone.* Oxford: Oxford University Press.

Barker, R. G., & Gump, P. V. (1964). *Big schools, small schools.* Stanford, CA: Stanford University Press.

Berliner, D. C. (2006). Our impoverished view of educational research. *Teachers College Record, 108*(6), 949–995.

Bernstein, J. (2006). *All together now: Common sense for a fair economy.* San Francisco: Berrett-Koehler.

Bishop, J. (1989). Why the apathy in American high schools? *Educational Researcher, 18*(1), 6–10, 42.

Brighouse, H. (2000). *School choice and social justice.* Oxford: Oxford University Press.

Brown v. Board of Education, 347 U.S. 483 (1954).

Bryk, A. S., Lee, V. E., & Holland, P. B. (1993). *Catholic schools and the common good.* Cambridge, MA: Harvard University Press.

Bryk, A. S., Sebring, P. B., Kerbow, D., Rollow, S., & Easton, J. Q. (1998). *Charting Chicago school reform.* Boulder, CO: Westview Press.

Camic, C., Gorski, P. S., & Trubek, D. M. (Eds.). (2005). *Max Weber's economy and society: A critical companion.* Palo Alto, CA Stanford University Press

Chubb, J. E. (1988). Why the current wave of school reform will fail. *Public Interest, 90,* 28–49.

Coaltion of Essential Schools. (2006). *The common principles.* Retrieved November 5, 2006, from http://www.essentialschools.org/pub/ces_docs/about/phil/10cps/10cps.html

Coleman, J. S. (1968). The concept of equality of educational opportunity. *Harvard Educational Review, 38,* 7–22.

Coleman, J. S. (1974). *Youth: Transition to adulthood: Report of the panel on youth of the President's science advisory committee.* Chicago: University of Chicago Press.

Coleman, J. S., & Hoffer, T. (1987). *Public and private schools: The impact of communities.* New York: Basic Books.

Cotton, K. (1996). *School size, school climate, and student performance.* Portland, OR: Northwest Regional Educational Laboratory.

Cotton, K. (2001). *New small learning communities: Findings from recent literature.* Portland, OR: Northwest Regional Educational Laboratory.

Darling-Hammond, L. (1985). Valuing teachers: The making of a profession. *Teachers College Record, 8*(2), 205–218.

Dewey, J. (1916). *Democracy and education.* New York: Macmillan Company.

Edmonds, R. (1979). Effective school for the urban poor. *Educational Leadership, 37,* 15–24.

Edwards v. Aguillard, 482 U.S. 578 (1987).

Friedman, M. (1962). *Capitalism and freedom.* Chicago: University of Chicago Press.

Fuhrman, S. H. (Ed.). (1993). *Designing coherent educational policy.* San Francisco: Jossey-Bass.

Fukuyama, F. (1999, May). The great disruption. *Atlantic Monthly, 283,* 55–80.

Gabarino, J. (1995). *Raising children in a socially toxic environment.* San Francisco, CA: Jossey-Bass.

Galston, W. (1991). *Liberal purposes.* Cambridge: Cambridge University Press.

Goals 2000: Educate American Act, 20 U.S.C. Sec. 5801 *et seq.* (1994).

Green, T. (1999). *Voices: The educational formation of conscience.* South Bend, IN: University of Notre Dame Press.

Gutmann, A. (1987). *Democratic education.* Princeton, NJ: Princeton University Press.

Hirsch, E. D., & Trefil, J. S. (1987). *Cultural literacy: What every American needs to know.* Boston: Houghton Mifflin.

Howley, C. (2002). Small schools. In A. Molnar (Ed.), *School reform proposals: The research evidence* (pp. 49–77). Greenwich, CT: Information Age.

Hoxby, C., & Murarka, S. (2007). *Charter schools in New York City: Who enrolls and how they affect their students' achievement.* Cambridge, MA: National Bureau of Economic Research.

Jacoby, S. (2008). *The age of American unreason.* New York: Pantheon.

Jenkins, J. M., & Keefe, J. W. (2002). Two schools: Two approaches to personalized learning. *Phi Delta Kappan 83*(6), 449–456.

Kahne, J. (2008). *Values and evidence: The academic and civic impact of small high school reform in Chicago.* Chicago: Spencer Foundation.

Kahne, J., Sporte, S., De la Torre, M., & Easton, J. (2008). Small high schools on a larger scale: The impact of school conversions in Chicago. *Educational Evaluation and Policy Analysis, 30*(3), 281–315.

Kitzmiller et al. v. Dover Area School District et al. United States District Court for the Middle District of Pennsylvania. December 20, 2005.

Klein, S. P., Hamilton, L. S., McCaffrey, D. F., & Stecher, B. M. (2000). What do test scores in Texas tell us? *Education Policy Analysis Archives, 8*(49), 2–23.

Kuhn, T. (1970). *The structure of scientific revolutions.* Chicago: University of Chicago Press.

Ladd, H. F. (2007). *Holding Schools Accountable Revisited.* Washington, DC: Association for Public Policy Analysis and Management.

Lee, V. E., & Ready, D. D. (2007). *Schools within schools: Possibilities and pitfalls of high school reform.* New York: Teachers College Press.

Lee, V. E., & Smith, J. B. (1997). High school size: Which works best, and for whom? *Educational Evaluation and Policy Analysis, 19*(3), 205–227.

Locke, J. (1946). *A letter concerning toleration* (J.W. Gough, Ed.). Oxford: Basil Blackwell. (Original work published 1689)

Locke, J. (1960). *Two treatises of government* (P. Laskett, Ed.). Cambridge: Cambridge University Press. (Original work published 1689)

Locke, J. (1964). *John Locke on education* (P. Guy, Ed.). New York: Teachers College Press. (Original work published 1693)

Macedo, S. (2000). *Diversity and distrust.* Cambridge, MA: Harvard University Press.

MacIntyre, A. (1981). *After virtue.* Notre Dame, IN: University of Notre Dame Press.

Mansbridge, J. (1980). *Beyond adversary democracy.* New York: Basic Books.

McQuillan, P. J. (2008). Small-school reform through the lens of complexity theory: It's "good to think with." *Teachers College Record, 110*(9), 1772–1801.

Meier, D. (2000). *Will standards save public education?* Boston: Beacon Press.

Meier, D. (2002a). *In schools we trust: Creating communities of learning in an era of testing and standardization.* Boston: Beacon Press.

Meier, D. (2002b). *The power of their ideas.* Boston: Beacon Press.

Mill, J. S. (1961). *Utilitarianism.* In J. Bentham & J. S. Mill, *The utilitarians.* Garden City, NY: Doubleday.

Mitchell, K., Shkolnik, J., Song, M., Uekawa, K., Murphy, R., Garet, M., et al. (2005). *Rigor, relevance, and results: The quality of teacher assignments and student work in new and conventional high schools.* Washington, DC: American Institutes for Research; Menlo Park, CA: SRI International.

Monk, D. H. (1990). *Educational finance: An economic approach.* New York: McGraw Hill.

Nagel, T. (1986). *The view from nowhere.* New York: Oxford University Press.

Nathan, J. (2008). *Small schools . . . should they be a big priority?* Chicago: Spencer Foundation.

Nathan, J., & Febey, K. (2001). *Smaller, safer, saner successful schools.* Minneapolis, MI: Center for School Change.

National Assessment of Educational Progress (NAEP). (2004). Trends in academic progress: three decades of student performance in reading and mathematics. Available online: http://nces.ed.gov/pubsearch/pubsinfo.asp?pubid=2005464

National Center for Education Statistics (NCES). (2000). Dropout rates in the United States 2000. Available online: http://nces.ed.gov/pubs2002/2002114.pdf

National Center for Education Statistics (NCES). (2007). High school dropout and completion rates in the United States. Available online: http://nces.ed.gov/pubs2009/2009064.pdf

National Commission on Excellence in Education. (1983). *A nation at risk.* Washington, DC: U.S. Department of Education.

A new compact for learning: A partnership to improve educational results in New York state. (1991). Albany: University of the State of New York, State Education Department.

Nichols, S. L., & Berliner, D. C. (2007a). *Collateral damage: How high-stakes testing corrupts America's schools.* Cambridge, MA: Harvard Education Press.

Nichols, S. L., & Berliner, D. C. (2007b/March/April). High-stakes testing and the corruption of America's schools. *Harvard Education Letter, 23*(2), 6–7.

No Child Left Behind Act of 2001. Pub. L. No. 107-110, 115 Stat. 1424 (2002).

Noddings, N. (1996). On community. *Educational Theory, 46*(3), 245–268.

Nussbaum, M. (1990). Aristotelian social democracy. In R. B. Douglass, G. M. Mara, & H. S. Richardson (Eds.), *Liberalism and the good* (pp. 203–252). New York: Routledge.

Nussbaum, M. (1997). *Cultivating humanity: A classical defense of reform in liberal education.* Cambridge, MA: Harvard University Press.

O'Day, J. A., & Smith, M. S. (1993). Systemic reform and educational opportunity. In S. H. Fuhrman (Ed.), *Designing Coherent Educational Policy* (pp. 250–312). San Francisco: Jossey-Bass.

Parents v. Seattle, 127 S. Ct. 2738 (2007).

Peshkin, A. (1986). *God's choice.* Chicago: University of Chicago Press.

Powell, A. G., Farrar, E., & Cohen, D. K. (1985). The Shopping Mall High School: Winners and Losers in the Educational Marketplace. New York: Houghton Mifflin.

Putnam, R. D. (1995). Bowling alone: America's declining social capital. *Journal of Democracy, 6*(1), 65–78.

Quint, J. (2006). *Meeting five critical challenges of high school reform: Lessons from research on three reform models.* New York: MDPC.

Ravitch, D. (2008). *Bill Gates and his silver bullet.* Retrieved November 21, 2008, from http://www.forbes.com/2008/11/18/gates-foundation-schools-oped-cx_dr_1119ravitch.html

Rawls, J. (1971). *A theory of justice.* Cambridge, MA: Harvard University Press.

Rawls, J. (1993). *Political liberalism.* New York: Columbia University Press.

Rawls, J. (1999). The idea of public reasons revisited. In *The law of peoples.* Cambridge, MA: Harvard University Press.

Raywid, M. A. (1996). *Taking stock: The movement to create mini-schools, schools within schools, and seperate small schools.* Madison, WI: Center on Organization and Restructuring of Schools.

Raywid, M. A. (1997). Successful school downsizing. *The School Administrator, 54*(9), 18–20, 22–23.

Raywid, M. A. (1999). *Current literature on small schools.* Retrieved September 25, 2006, from http://www.ericdigests.org/1999-3/small.htm

Raywid, M. A., & Osiyama, L. (2000). Musings in the wake of Columbine: What can schools do? *Phi Delta Kappan, 81*(6), 444–449.

Raywid, M. A., & Schmerler, G. (2003). *Not so easy going: The policy environment of small urban schools and schools-within-schools.* Charleston, WV: AEL.

Rhodes, D., Smerdon, B., Burt, W., Evan, A., Martinez, B., & Means., B. (2005). *Getting to results: Student outcomes in new and redesigned high schools.* Washington, DC: American Institutes for Research; Menlo Park, CA: SRI International.

Rorty, R. (1981). The priority of democracy to philosophy. In *Objectivity, relativism, and truth.* Cambridge: Cambridge University Press.

Rothstein, R. (2002). *Out of balance: Our understanding of how schools affect society and how society affects schools.* Chicago: Spencer Foundation.

Rothstein, R. (2004). *Class and schools: Using social, economic, and educational reform to close the black-white achievement gap.* New York: Teachers College Press.

Rothstein, R., Jacobson, R., & Wilder, T. (2008). *Grading education: Getting accountability right.* Washington, DC: Economic Policy Institute; New York: Teachers College Press.

Rousseau, J.-J. (1911). *Émile: ou, De l'education.* Paris: J. Gillequin. (Original work published 1762)

Sandel, M. (1982). *Liberalism and the limits of justice.* Cambridge: Cambridge University Press.

Sergiovanni, T. (1992). *Moral leadership.* San Francisco: Jossey-Bass.

Shanker, A. (1994). National standards. In C. E. Finn, Jr. & H. J. Walberg (Eds.), *Radical education reform* (pp. 3–20). Berkeley, CA: McCutchan.

Shear, L., Means, B., Mitchell, K., House, A., Gorges, T., Joshi, A., et al. (2008). Contrasting paths to small-school reform: Results of a 5-year evaluation of the Bill & Melinda Gates Foundation's national high schools initiative. *Teachers College Record,110*(9), 1986–2039.

Shouse, R. C. (1996). Academic press and sense of community: Conflict and congruence in American high schools. *Research in Sociology of Education and Socialization, 11*, 173–202.

Sizer, T. (1984). *Horace's compromise: The dilemma of the American high school.* New York: Houghton Mifflin

Small Schools Project. (2009). *Personalization.* Retrieved August 23, 2009, from http://www.smallschoolsproject.org/index.asp?siteloc=whysmall&section=personal

Smith, A. (2000). *The wealth of nations.* New York: Modern Library. (Original work published 1776)

Stell et al. v. Savannah 333 F.2d 55 (5th Cir. 1964).

Stout, J. (1988). *Ethics after Babel.* Boston, MA: Beacon Press.

Stout, J. (2004). *Democracy and tradition.* Princeton, NJ: Princeton University Press.

Strike, K. A. (1979). An epistemology of practical research. *Educational Researchers, 8*(1), 10–16.

Strike, K. A. (1981). Toward a moral theory of desegregation. In J. Soltis (Ed.), *Philosophy and education: Eightieth yearbook of the national society for the study of education* (pp. 213–235). Chicago: University of Chicago Press.

Strike, K. A. (1990). Is teaching a profession: How would we know? *Journal of Personnel Evaluation in Education, 4*, 91–117.

Strike, K. A. (1993). Professionalism, democracy, and discursive communities: Normative reflections on restructuring. *American Educational Research Journal, 30*(2), 255–275.

Strike, K. A. (1997). Centralized goal formation and systemic reform: Reflections on liberty, localism and pluralism. *Educational Policy Analysis Archives, 5*(11). Retrieved September 2, 2009, from http://epaa/asu/epaa/v5n11.html

Strike, K. A. (1999). Can schools be communities? The tension between shared values and inclusion. *Educational Administration Quarterly, 35*(1), 46–70.

Strike, K. A. (2005). Is liberal education illiberal? Political liberalism and liberal education. In *Philosophy of education, 2004* (pp. 321–129). Urbana, IL: Philosophy of Education Society.

Strike, K. A. (2008). Equality of opportunity and school finance: A commentary on Ladd, Satz and Brighouse and Swift. *Education Finance and Policy, 3*(4), 467–494.

Strike, K. A., & Serow, R. C. (1978). How tolerant are high school students? *Educational Forum, 42*, 327–336.

Toch, T. (2003). *High schools on a human scale*. Boston: Beacon Press.

Tonnies, F. (1988). *Community and society* (C. Loomis, Trans.). New Brunswick: Transaction Books.

Vander Ark, T. (2002). Personalization: Making every school a small school. *Principal Leadership, 2*(6), 10–14.

Walzer, M. (1995). The communitarian critique of liberalism. In A. Etzioni (Ed.), *New communitarian thinking*. Charlottesville, VA: University of Virginia Press.

Wasley, P. A., Fine, M., Gladden, M., Holland, N. E., King, S. P., Mosak, E., et al. (2000). *Small schools: Great strides*. New York: Bank Street College of Education.

Wisconsin v. Yoder, 406 U. S. 205 (1972).

Wittgenstein, L. (1986). *Philosophical investigations* (3rd ed.). New York: Macmillan. (Original work published 1953)

Wyse, A. E., Keesler, V., & Schneider, B. (2008). Assessing the effects of small school size on mathematics achievement: A propensity score-matching approach. *Teachers College Record, 110*(9), 1879–1900.

Young, I. M. (2000). *Inclusion and democracy*. Oxford: Oxford University Press.

Young math competitors honor a hero. (2001, July 15). *New York Times*, p. 12.

Index

democratic communities and, 73–75
externalities, 74
justice and, 74–75
nature of, 73–75
public goods versus, 74–75
of school in community, 75
Common Principles of Coalition of
  Essential Schools, 55–56, 63–65, 70,
  79, 95, 106, 160
Communication
  communicative justice, 78–79
  intergenerational, 20–21
Communicative justice, 78–79
Communitarianism, 28–31
  of free school movement, 39–40
  individualism versus, 101–104, 106
  nature of, 28
  in small schools, 101–104
Community. *See also* Caring communities;
  Community-based reform;
  Democratic communities; Intellectual
  communities
  alienation versus, 28, 34, 62–63
  authentic teaching and learning and,
    1–4, 17–22, 54–55, 63–65, 70, 122
  challenges of, 22–27, 159
  communitarian critique of liberalism
    and, 28–31
  connection and, 50, 52–53, 64–65
  creation of, 3
  decline of, in modernity, 22–25
  "four Cs" of, 50–53, 63–65, 79
  human capital formation and, 8, 27, 33,
    40, 49, 131–132, 159
  importance of, 1–4, 17–22
  in learning a subject, 41–45
  liberalism and, 26, 27, 28–31
  metaphors for, 31–33, 44
  as missing element of school reform,
    xiii–xv
  in modernity, 22–25
  moral authority of, 29–30, 80–81, 134
  nature of, xvi–xvii
  need for, 1–4, 17–22
  negative aspects of, 31–33, 80–82

normation and, 28, 29, 38–45, 62, 133,
  136
partial communities, 9–10, 22, 81, 157
of practice. *See* Intellectual
  communities
quality of, 14
reconstituting across generations,
  51–52
role of standards in undermining, 7–8
schools that are communities, 36
schools that are not communities,
  33–35
as shared educational project, 4, 24,
  46–50, 130
small schools and, 8–14, 162
"thick," 23–24, 31, 32
total communities, 4, 31, 81
Community-based reform
  accountability and, 134, 136, 151–155
  assumptions, 129, 136
  curriculum in, 132
  described, 135–137
  educational goals and, 131–132, 136
  governance and organizational
    structure in, 133
  moral norms in, 134
  motivation and, 130, 135, 136
Compartmentalization, 49
Comprehensive schools, 10, 11, 49, 79, 91
Connection
  adult-child relationships, 52
  in communities, 50, 52–53, 64–65
  flat organizational structure, 52
  intergenerational closure, 52
  scale in, 52
  stability, 52–53
Constitution of the United States, 28–29
Consumer sovereignty, 127–128, 131–132
Contract. *See* Social contract
Core Knowledge Curriculum, 98
Cotton, Kathleen, 87, 89, 92, 96, 107
Crew, Rudy, 88, 98, 99
Critical thinking, developing capacity for,
  4, 71
Cultural transmission, 28

About the Author

Kenneth A. Strike is Professor of Cultural Foundations at Syracuse University and Professor Emeritus of Education at Cornell University. He has a Ph.D. from Northwestern University. He has also taught at the University of Wisconsin and was a department chair at the University of Maryland. His research emphasizes professional ethics and political philosophy as it applies to matters of educational policy. He has authored, coauthored, or edited over a dozen books and about 150 articles and book chapters. He is a past president of the Philosophy of Education Society and has been elected a member of the National Academy of Education.